The Ethics of Redistribution

D0980811

A Liberty*Press* Edition

LIBERTY FUND
LIBRARY OF THE PHILOSOPHY OF LIBERTY

The Servile State
Hilaire Belloc

Liberty, Equality, Fraternity
James Fitzjames Stephen

The Limits of State Action
Wilhelm von Humboldt

Democracy and Liberty
William Hartpole Lecky

A Plea for Liberty
Thomas Mackay, ed.

Envy
Helmut Schoeck

The Man Versus the State
Herbert Spencer

On Liberty, Society, and Politics
William Graham Sumner

Bertrand de Jouvenel

The Ethics of Redistribution

INTRODUCTION BY JOHN GRAY

Liberty Fund

Indianapolis
1990

Introduction © 1990 by John Gray. All rights reserved. All inquiries should be addressed to Liberty Fund, Inc., 8335 Allison Pointe Trail, Suite 300, Indianapolis, Indiana 46250-1687. This book was manufactured in the United States of America.

First published 1952. Reprinted with permission from Cambridge University Press.

Library of Congress Cataloging-in-Publication Data

Jouvenel, Bertrand de, 1903–1987
   The ethics of redistribution / by Bertrand de Jouvenel; introduction by John Gray.
     p.   cm.
   Reprint. Originally published: Cambridge: University Press, 1952.
   ISBN 0-86597-084-X. — ISBN 0-86597-085-8 (pbk.)
   1. Income distribution—Moral and ethical aspects.   2. Transfer payments—Moral and ethical aspects.   3. Social ethics.   4. Social justice.   I. Title.
HB523.J68   1989
339.2'2—dc20
                                             89-27759
                                               CIP

10 9 8 7 6 5 4 3

Contents

The theory of diminishing utility
Further points and qualifications
Discrimination against minorities
The effect of redistribution upon society
The more redistribution, the more power to the State
Values and satisfactions
Are subjective satisfactions an exclusive standard?
Redistributionism the end result of utilitarian individualism

Two views of income
Taxation not purely disincentive
Another view of income
Gnawing the income-bone
Conflict of subjective egalitarianism and objective socialism
Functional expenditures well received if charged to
    corporate bodies
The treatment of corporate bodies compared to that of
    families
Consumption expenditures as a form of national
    investment
Purposeful expenditures the State's privilege
A high degree of taxation in all ranges
The camouflage of personal expenditures
The destruction of free services
Commercialization of values
A redistribution of power from individuals to the State
Redistribution an incentive to tolerating the growth of
    public expenditure
Redistribution incidental to centralization?
Envy a fundamental motive?

Foreword

The Boutwood Lectures at Corpus Christi College were founded by Mary Boutwood in memory of her husband, Arthur Boutwood, a Civil Servant in the Charity Commission, but more widely known through his writings, usually under the pseudonym Hackeluyt Egerton, on the philosophy of religion and political philosophy.

The College was fortunate in securing Baron de Jouvenel to deliver the lectures in the autumn of 1949 and welcomed the suggestion made on behalf of the University Press that his lectures should be published. I am glad to have this opportunity of expressing our thanks to the lecturer, to the University Press, and, also, to Mrs. Patrick Bury who prepared the lectures for publication.

Corpus Christi College   Will Spens
2 October 1950

Preface

I feel honored that I was invited to give these lectures in Cambridge, and by the famous college of Corpus Christi, that they should now be published by the Cambridge University Press and introduced by Sir Will Spens. Would that the offering were worthier of such patrons!

Generous friends helped to deck it out, as a plain girl invited to an unwonted feast. Never has so slight a piece benefited by so much excellent advice.

Mr. and Mrs. Patrick Bury kindly eradicated my major errors of form, though they could not remedy the clumsiness attendant upon the use of a foreign language. Dr. Ronald F. Henderson, Professor Ely Devons of Manchester, and Professor Milton Friedman of Chicago read the proofs for economic barbarisms, Professor Willmoore Kendall of Yale read them as a political theorist.

It would be an ill return for their most generous help to saddle them with any responsibility for my views and the errors I may have persevered in.

I trust it will be clear to the reader that this little essay is in no way meant as a contribution to the great debate on income redistribution; but rather as an attempt to stress values commonly disregarded in this debate. Contributions to civilization cannot be rightly assessed in national income calculations.

9 May 1951   Bertrand de Jouvenel

Introduction

Bertrand de Jouvenel's study in the ethics of redistribution is distinctive, in the first instance, because it focuses precisely on the morality of redistribution and not on its side effects on incentives. This is to say that de Jouvenel's critique embodies a fundamental challenge to the values expressed in redistributionist thought which in no way depends upon an instrumental or utilitarian assessment of the consequences of redistributionist policy. De Jouvenel is concerned with the impact on individual liberty and on cultural life of redistribution rather than with its effects on productivity.

His study is significant for another reason, which is that he is careful to distinguish redistributionism from other, superficially similar doctrines. Thus, he shows clearly how it differs from agrarian egalitarianism, which aims to equalize a resource—land—but does not seek to control the distribution of its product. Again, redistributionism is not socialism. Redistributionism has caused severe harm to modern civilization but has not destroyed it. On the other hand, socialism is the suppression of private property in a new order of communal moral solidarity and is incompatible with modern society. It can be realized, if at all, only in monasteries where material goods are spurned or in communities that are small, simple, and even primitive—an insight that was grasped by Rousseau but not by Marx.

De Jouvenel makes another fundamental distinction within redistributionism itself. Modern redistributionism encompasses two wholly disparate elements: the belief that government should be centrally involved in the relief of poverty, and the belief that economic inequality is itself unjust or evil. These two beliefs have indeed been conflated in the increasing acceptance of the view that it is the responsibility of government to ensure rising popular living standards. A further move in the direction of egalitarian redistributionism is taken when to the proposal that government supply a subsistence floor beneath which no one may fall is added the proposal that there be instituted a ceiling beyond which no one may rise.

As de Jouvenel shows, such egalitarian proposals are given specious support by the invocation of a felicific calculus which incorporates the claim that income has a diminishing marginal utility—a claim he criticizes incisively by showing the insuperable impediments to our making reliable comparisons of interpersonal satisfaction. De Jouvenel might also have noted that, even if utilities were interpersonally comparable, redistribution according to marginalist principles would have morally perverse results. It would sanction the redistribution of resources from the very worse-off (the depressed paraplegic, say) to those, chiefly in the middle range of income and natural endowments, who could generate most satisfaction from the resources. This is not a result congenial to egalitarian sentiment, but it flows inexorably from the marginalist argument for redistribution.

De Jouvenel's ethical critique of redistributionism is powerful and many-layered. He develops an important empirical criticism of egalitarian redistributionism when he observes that the resources needed to support a subsistence minimum cannot be derived solely, or even primarily, from taxation of the rich. Such resources must be extracted from the middle classes, who are also the beneficiaries of income-transfer schemes. This is a point of cardinal importance in de Jouvenel's critique. His insight that the distributional upshot of transfer schemes is extremely complex and sometimes regressive has been amply confirmed by more recent historical experience. He further notes that a policy of redistribution is bound to discriminate against minorities, since it will inevitably favor the preferences and interests of the majority—a fact remarked upon also by Hayek.

Redistributionist policy is condemned by de Jouvenel, in addition, for undermining the sense of personal responsibility. It does this by transferring authority for crucial life-decisions from the individuals who make them to the State. By catering for all the basic needs of the individual, the State leaves him with authority only in the sphere of determining how to spend his pocket money. Again, the effect of redistributionist policy is to disprivilege the family as against such legal fictions as the corporation—principally by conferring upon businesses tax immunities denied to families. The regime of high taxation inseparable from the redistributionist state has the further undesirable consequences of diminishing the sphere of free services in which people engage in convivial relations without the expectation of payment—and thereby corroding the culture of civility that sustains liberal civilization.

For de Jouvenel, however, the most profound result of redistributionist policy is the impetus it gives to the baleful process of centralization. If the state confiscates high incomes and imposes penal rates of taxation on saving and investment, the state must take over the saving and investment activities that private individuals are no longer able to undertake. If, because of the confiscation of higher incomes, there are important social and cultural activities that can no longer be sustained privately, such as provision for high culture and the arts, then once again the state must assume responsibility for such activities through a program of subsidy. Inevitably, the state comes to exercise an ever-increasing degree of control over them. The consequence of redistributionist policy, accordingly, is the curtailment of private initiative in many spheres of social life, the destruction of the man of independent means, and the weakening of civil society.

De Jouvenel goes on to speculate that the underlying causal process may go in the opposite direction: Redistributionist policy may be an incident in a process of centralization that has acquired a momentum of its own. Here de Jouvenel anticipates the findings of the Virginia School of Public Choice, most profoundly theorized in the work of James Buchanan,[1] which illuminate the origins of the expansionist state in the economic interests of government bureaucracies. As de Jouvenel, once again anticipating the insights of later theorists of the New Class, presciently concludes:

> We then may well wonder which of these two closely linked phenomena is predominant: whether it is redistribution or centralization. We may ask ourselves whether what we are dealing with is not a political even more than a social phenomenon. This political phenomenon consists in the demolition of the class enjoying "independent means" and in the massing of means in the hands of managers. This results in a transfer of power from individuals to officials, who tend to constitute a new ruling class as against that which is being destroyed. And there is a faint but quite perceptible trend toward immunity for this new class from some part of the fiscal measures directed at the former.

---

[1] See James M. Buchanan, *The Limits of Liberty: Between Anarchy and Leviathan* (Chicago: University of Chicago Press, 1975).

Subsequent thought and experience have strongly cor-
roborated de Jouvenel's perceptive account. Empirical research reveals the transfer payments schemes of the major Western democracies to be ruleless and chaotic.
Insofar as it is the creation of redistributionist ideology,
the modern welfare state is not defensible by reference to
any coherent set of principles or purposes. It has not significantly alleviated poverty but has instead substantially
institutionalized it. This is the upshot of pathbreaking
studies such as Charles Murray's *Losing Ground*.[2] A generation of welfare policy has inflicted on its clients such
disincentives and moral hazards as to leave their last
state worse than their first. The net, on-balance impact of
the entire array of redistributional measures conforms to
no clear pattern (save that, as Nozick has noted,[3] if any
social group benefits it is likely to be the middle class majority rather than the poor). And Hayek's conjecture in
The Constitution of Liberty that the redistributionist state is
bound to be an expansionist state, like de Jouvenel's ear-
lier warning, has been increasingly borne out by events.

Recent developments in philosophical inquiry confirm
the essential soundness of de Jouvenel's analysis. Robert
Nozick's *Anarchy, State and Utopia* contains a critique of
the idea of social or distributive justice that parallels
closely de Jouvenel's criticism of the ethics of redistribution. Nozick's attack, like de Jouvenel's, has several elements or layers. He shows, first, that the attempt to impose an approved pattern on the social distribution of
goods requires continuous interference with individual
liberty, since gifts and free exchange will constantly sub-
vert the pattern. As Nozick famously put it, the end re-

[2] Charles Murray, *Losing Ground: American Social Policy 1950–1980* (New York, Basic Books, 1985).

[3] Robert Nozick, *Anarchy, State and Utopia* (New York: Basic Books, 1974).

sult of the attempt to impose a pattern on distribution is a socialist state that forbids capitalist acts among consenting adults.

Redistributionist policy embodies an abstract or false individualism in which the intermediary institutions that are the indispensable matrix of individuality are neglected or suppressed. It is especially hostile to the institution that is the cornerstone of civil society—the family. Nozick follows de Jouvenel in noting that the institution of the family is disprivileged under any redistributionist regime: "To such views, families are disturbing; for within a family occur transfers that upset the favored distribution."[4]

It is in the more recent work of Hayek that de Jouvenel's analysis is most strikingly paralleled. In the second volume of his trilogy *Law, Legislation and Liberty*, entitled *The Mirage of Social Justice*,[5] Hayek develops a devastating critique of current distributive conceptions that strengthens, and extends in directions that are thoroughly innovative, the central thrust of de Jouvenel's analysis. Hayek's first and perhaps most radically original thesis is that no government or central authority can know enough to be able to realize or impose the preferred distributional pattern. This is true, whether the distributional principles refer to the satisfaction of basic needs, linking rewards to merits, realizing equality of resources or well-being, or whatever. Whatever the distributional principles, the knowledge needed to implement them is, except in a few limiting cases, so dispersed throughout society and so often in tacit or practical form that it is usually impossible for government to collect it in any usable form. This irretrievable dispersion or division

---

[4] Ibid., p. 167.

[5] F.A. Hayek, *Law, Legislation and Liberty, Volume Two: The Mirage of Social Justice* (Chicago: University of Chicago Press, 1976).

of knowledge in society erects an insuperable epistemic barrier to the realization of virtually all contemporary distributivist conceptions. It renders unrealizable even the most subtle of them, that of John Rawls,[6] inasmuch as government could never have sufficient information to know whether the Difference Principle (requiring that inequality be restricted to that which is necessary to maximize the holdings of the worst-off) has been satisfied.

There is a second strand of argument in *The Mirage of Social Justice* that strengthens de Jouvenel's case against redistribution. This is the claim that, even were government able to acquire the knowledge needed to implement its preferred distributional principles, there exists no consensus in society as to how the different principles are to be weighted when they come into conflict with one another. If, for example, the satisfaction of basic needs competes with rewarding merit, which is to be given priority? Since our society contains no overarching moral code in terms of which such considerations may be compared, they are for us incommensurable, in regard to which there exists no agreed procedure of rational arbitration. For this reason, any allocation of resources according to a weighing of these values cannot avoid appearing, and indeed being, unprincipled, unpredictable, and arbitrary. Because of such inevitable conflicts among its constitutive values, redistributionism cannot fail to spawn bureaucracies with wide discretionary powers. But the large margin of discretionary authority exercised by the apparatus of redistribution is difficult to reconcile with the institution of the rule of law that is one of the foundations of a free society.

There is a final strand in Hayek's argument that links it with the analyses of de Jouvenel by James Buchanan. This is the proposition that, in the absence of any princi-

---

[6] John Rawls, *A Theory of Justice* (Cambridge: Belknap Press of the Harvard University Press, 1971).

pled justification of redistributional policy, it is best theorized in terms of its beneficiaries. Redistributionism then comes to be intelligible as a system of ideas whose function is to legitimate the interests of expansionist bureaucracies and, in general, to insulate well-established interest groups from the negative side-effects of economic change. Redistributionism thus emerges, at last, as the conservative ideology of the interventionist state and its client groups.

Though *The Ethics of Redistribution* is remarkably contemporary in many of its insights, de Jouvenel himself was never completely satisfied with it. In a letter of 18 September 1981, he wrote: "As to my *Ethics of Redistribution*, I have repeatedly refused its reprint. I have dwelt upon the subject in the many years gone by and I now have to say, not only what I then thought, but what I have acquired since. . . ." He never returned to this work and died on 1 March 1987 at the age of 83.

This seminal little work remains extraordinarily fertile and suggestive of further thought and inquiry as we can see from its many points of affinity with the more recent work of Buchanan, Hayek, Nozick, Rawls, and others. It is an important contribution to discussion about the redistributionist state and its implications for liberty. Its republication is to be welcomed.

John Gray
Fellow of Jesus College
Oxford

Work on this Foreword was conducted by the author during a period of residence as Stranahan Distinguished Research Fellow at the Social Philosophy and Policy Center, Bowling Green State University, Ohio.

The Ethics of Redistribution

Lecture I

The Socialist Ideal

I propose to discuss a predominant preoccupation of our day: the redistribution of incomes.

The process of redistribution

In the course of a lifetime, current ideas as to what may be done in a society by political decision have altered radically. It is now generally regarded as within the proper province of the State, and indeed as one of its major functions, to shift wealth from its richer to its poorer members. "An exceedingly complex machinery has grown up piecemeal"[1] to provide money benefits, free services, goods and services below cost. This machinery is more extensive than that of public finance, however enlarged, as in the operation of rent control. Its purpose is to redistribute incomes and especially, it is generally assumed, the incomes of the richer, which are drained by progressive taxation and at the same time affected by rent control, limitation of dividends, and requisition of assets.

The whole process seems to have taken its impetus in this country exactly forty years ago with Lloyd George's budget for 1909–10, which, in introducing progressive taxation, abandoned the idea that for taxation purposes, equality implies proportionality. The same Chancellor introduced the first sickness and employment benefit schemes. It is to be noticed that "the policy of bringing about a more egalitarian distribution of income by public finance"[2] and by complementary means, which is now so clearly stated as a rule of conduct, has emerged from the

[1] James Edward Meade, *Planning and the Price Mechanism* (London, 1948), p. 42.
[2] Ursula K. Hicks, *Public Finance* (London, 1947), p. 146.

5

process itself. It does not seem to have started as a grand design. Circumstances, above all the two great wars, and social pressures, sustained by strong moral emotion, have brought us gradually to a point where an ethical purpose can be stated: As against previous or extra-western ideals, the West is fast adopting the ideal of the equalization of incomes by State action.

Our subject: the ethical aspect

A spirited controversy is now raging on what is termed "the disincentive effect of excessive redistribution." It is known from experience that in most cases, though by no means in all, men are spurred by material rewards pro-portional or even more than proportional to their effort, as for example in "time and a half." Making each in-crease of effort less rewarding than those which preceded it, while at the same time lowering, by the provision of benefits, the basic effort necessary to sustain existence, can be held to affect the pace of production and economic progress. Thus, the policy of redistribution is subject to heavy fire. The attack, however, is made on grounds of expediency. Current criticism of redistribution is not based on its being undesirable but on its being, beyond a certain point, imprudent. Nor do champions of redistri-bution deny that there are limits to what can be achieved, if it is proposed, as they wish, to maintain economic progress. This whole conflict of which so much is made today is a borderline quarrel, involving no fundamentals.

I propose to skirt this field of combat and shall assume here that redistribution, however far it may be carried, exerts no disincentive influence and leaves the volume and growth of production entirely unaffected. This as-sumption is made in order to center attention upon other aspects of redistribution. To some the assumption may seem to do away with the need for discussion. If it were not going to affect production, they will say, redistribution would have to proceed to its extreme of total equality of incomes. This would be good and desirable. But would it? Why would it? And how far would it? This is my starting point.

Dealing with redistribution purely on ethical grounds, our first concern must be to distinguish sharply between the social ideal of income equalization and others with which it is sentimentally, but not logically, associated. It is a common but ill-founded belief that ideals of social reform are somehow lineal descendants of one another. It is not so: Redistributionism is not descended from socialism; nor can any but a purely verbal link be discovered between it and agrarian egalitarianism. It will greatly clarify the problem if we stress the contrasts between these ideals.

Land redistribution in perspective

What was demanded in the name of social justice over thousands of years was land redistribution. This may be said to belong to a past phase of history when agriculture was by far the major economic activity. Yet the agrarian demand comes right down to our own times: Did not the First World War bring in its train an ample redistribution of land over all of Eastern Europe? Was not the cry of land redistribution Lenin's chief slogan in Russia, though used with a view to promoting a very different revolution? Again, should we not remember that land redistribution in East Prussia was a major issue at the end of the Weimar Republic, and that Brüning fell for much the same reason as the elder Gracchus? Thus, the idea should not appear to us as an archaeological curiosity. It is with us to this day, it agitates Italy at this moment;[3] and, as we shall see, the feeling which lends it strength is a basic one in social ethics.

It is the idea that all men should be equally endowed with natural resources from which to draw produce (i.e., income) in proportion to their toil.

There is authority for it in the Bible. In the first instance land is to be apportioned by lots[4] and any emergent inequality in the holdings is to be redressed at the jubilee, when each seller of land is to be restored in possession of the lot he alienated.[5] This return to the initial position every forty-nine years precludes the formation of *latifundia* and restores equality of land holdings between families. The ideal of entailed holdings for members of families related by blood or name, however accounted for, is a fundamental one in ancient Indo-European society. With it there generally goes the practice of frequent redistribution of strips according to numbers within the group. Thus, the claims of agrarian reformers seem to have rested upon age-old tradition and to have appealed to an ancestral feeling of rightness.

Land redistribution not equivalent to redistribution of income

There is a clear contrast between redistribution of land and redistribution of incomes. Agrarianism does not advocate the equalization of the produce, but of natural resources out of which the several units will autonomously

---

[3] 1949.
[4] Num. 33:54.
[5] Lev. 25:28.

provide themselves with the produce. This is justice, in the sense that inequality of rewards between units equally provided with natural resources will reflect inequality of toil. In other words, the role played by inequality of "capital" in bringing about unequal rewards is nullified. What is equalized is the supply of "capital."

Now the idea of eliminating the influence of capital from functions determining income is not an archaic one: It runs right through social thought at all times. When Marx said that value was made up of labor only, he was in fact resorting by wishful thinking to a state of affairs which seems inherently right. That the idea of rewards in proportion to the contribution made was a basic one with the classical economists is plain enough: They were concerned to show that this would be the outcome of a perfectly competitive system, and to them the initial distribution of property was always a disturbing factor.

Agrarian reformers are often claimed by the socialists as their forerunners. They are not; but the two groups do have one preoccupation in common: Both want to eliminate the effect of an unequal distribution of property.

This, of course, does not imply—even on the assumption of a strictly equal initial supply of capital—any equality of incomes. These would anyhow follow the well-known laws of dispersion. Drawing a curve, the abscissae of which represent the amount of incomes and the ordinates the number of economic units enjoying these amounts, we should obtain the well-known Gaussian bell-shaped curve but, as Professor Pigou points out,[6] without the skewness given to this curve by the unequal distribution of property. Thus, the agrarian principle is fair reward and not equality of incomes.

[6] A.C. Pigou, *The Economics of Welfare* (London, 1920), pp. 650–51 of 1948 ed.

Equalization of land assets: how far similar to and how far different from equalization of capital

We have been led to reformulate the agrarian principle in modern terms as demanding equalization of the supply of capital. However, that is a generalization which tends to distort what agrarian reformers have in fact historically claimed. They thought in terms of land redistribution and were usually chary of including among the things to be redistributed such capital assets (as we should call them) as tools or equipment. Although a complete redistribution would seem called for to ensure that rewards are related strictly to immediate achievement, they were prone to exclude tools. Perhaps this was due to an essential difference perceived between "natural resources" and "capital." Land (and this applies to natural resources in general) was thought of as offered by God to men, not to be engrossed by any of their number, while tools are man-made and can legitimately be passed on. It may perhaps be regarded as significant that in many primitive communities the transfer of land can only be effected by the transfer with it of some very personal object, as if in this way it might assume the characteristics of personal property,[7] though it is not so by nature.

Thus, agrarian egalitarianism may be said to embody two notions: one that natural resources are not to be engrossed, the other that fair rewards can be obtained only when the supply of capital is evenly spread out. These notions are far from irrelevant in the modern world. The former was invoked only recently by Mussolini, when he

[7] The seisin would consist among the Veddas of a flint and steel, of a tooth (C.G. Seligmann and Brenda Seligmann, *The Veddas*, Cambridge, 1911, pp. 113–17), or of a stone, which may be taken to deputize for a piece of personal property. Similar types of seisin are found in many primitive societies.

proclaimed the right of the poorer nations to an equal share in the world's natural resources: That this proved to be an effective propaganda theme testifies that the idea is deeply ingrained. Furthermore, the feeling that the true way to social justice lies in some redistribution of capital is the basic ingredient of all reforming schemes set up against the collectivist program. These seek to make the agrarian principle applicable to modern societies; this is what Chesterton advocated. The secret of achieving it in practice has not been found, but many confused strivings[8] testify that the old concept is very much alive. Indeed, it will never pall.

Socialism as the City of Brotherly Love

Agrarianism can be summed up under the heading of *fair rewards*. Socialism aims even higher than the establishment of "mere" justice. It seeks to establish a new order of brotherly love. The basic socialist feeling is not that things are out of proportion and thus unjust, that reward is not proportional to effort, but an emotional revolt against the antagonisms within society, against the ugliness of men's behavior to each other.

It is of course logically possible to minimize antagonism by minimizing the occasions on which men's paths cross. Thus, the agrarian solution lies in the economic sovereignty of each several owner on his well-delimited field, which is equal in size to that of his neighbor. But this is not possible in modern societies, where interests are intertwined as in a Gordian knot. To cut the knot means reversion to a ruder state. But there is another solution: It is a new spirit of joyful acceptance of this inter-

---

[8] "A property-owning democracy."

dependence; it is that men, called to serve one another ever increasingly by economic progress and division of labor, should do so "in newness of spirit,"[9] not as the "old" man did who grudgingly measured his service against his reward, but as a "new" man who finds his delight in the welfare of his brethren.

The pattern is easily recognizable: It is the Pauline pattern of law and grace, as transformed by Rousseau. For Rousseau, social progress increases strife: It arouses man's desires, and, as he comes to stand in too close propinquity to his fellows, his self-love is turned into wickedness because he finds that they do not serve him enough or that they hinder him too much. Rousseau's answer to this, an answer which he believed to be valid only if introduced as a preventive and never as a cure,[10] was the displacement of man's center of affections, love of the whole being substituted for self-love. This is the fundamental pattern of socialist thought. It is from Rousseau again that socialism derives its belief that social antagonism arises from "objective situations," the removal of which should remove strife. And socialism has singled out private property as the basic "situation" creating antagonisms: It creates first the essential antagonism between those with property and those without, and second the struggle among the propertied.

How to do away with antagonism: socialist goal and socialist means

The socialist solution, then, is the destruction of private property as such. This is to erase the contrast between

[9] Rom. 7:6.

[10] See my "Essai sur la Politique de Rousseau," in introduction to my critical edition of *Du Contrat Social* (Geneva, 1946).

men's positions and thereby do away with tension. The proletariat, made conscious of its solidarity in its struggle to do away with property, will, when victorious, absorb into itself the now proletarianized remainder. Social antagonisms would thereby be extinguished and the force of repression formerly called for by the existence of antagonisms in order to preserve civil peace in an atmosphere of war, that is, the power of the State, will become unnecessary. This power must then of itself wither away.

This promise that the State will wither away is fundamental to socialist doctrine, because the disappearance of antagonisms is the fundamental aim of socialism; but it has somewhat suffered from being bandied about in political controversy. Some shrewd critics of socialism have very properly taken the withering away of the State as the criterion of socialist success, thereby causing annoyance to their opponents. In the dust of combat the fact that the State is expected to wither away as an instrument of repression and of police power has been somewhat lost sight of, and in fairness it does not seem that enlarged functions of the State, by themselves, prove a failure of socialism but only the preservation and *a fortiori* the enlargement of police powers. It is, however, only too evident that police powers are at their greatest where the destruction of private property has been most completely achieved—a plain fact which refutes socialist belief.

It is clear for all to see that the destruction of private property has not done away with antagonisms or given rise to a spirit of solidarity permitting men to dispense with police powers; and it is further apparent that what spirit of solidarity there is seems to have as its necessary ingredient the distrust and hatred of another society, or of another section of society. The warlike intentions of foreign powers seem to be a basic postulate of the collectivist State and may even be attributed by one collectivist State to another or, if the process of socialization has not been completed, to the aggressive disposition of the capital classes, backed by foreign capitalists. Thus, the solidarity obtained is not, as intended, a solidarity of love but, at least in part, a solidarity in strife. Clearly, this is not consonant with the basic intention of socialism: "the fruit of righteousness is sown in peace of them that make peace."[11]

Yet the socialist ideal is not to be summarily dismissed. We do aspire to something more than a society of good neighbors who do not displace landmarks, who return stray sheep to their owner, and who refrain from coveting their neighbor's ass. And indeed a community based not upon economic independence but upon a fraternal partaking of the common produce, and inspired by the deep-seated feeling that its members are of one family, should not be called utopian.

The inner contradiction of socialism

Such a community works. It has worked for centuries, and we can see it at work under our very eyes in every monastic community. But it is to be noticed that these are cities of brotherly love *because* they were originally cities built up by love of the Father. It is further to be noticed that material goods are shared without question *because* they are spurned. The members of the community are not anxious to increase their individual well-being at the expense of one another, but then they are not very anxious to increase it *at all*. Their appetites are not addressed to scarce material commodities, and thus compet-

[11] James 3:18.

itive; they are addressed to God, who is infinite. In short, they are members of one another not because they form a social body but because they are part of a mystical body.

Socialism seeks to restore this unity without the faith which causes it. It seeks to restore sharing as among brothers without contempt for worldly goods, without recognition of their worthlessness. It does not accept the view that consumption is a trivial thing, to be kept down to the minimum. On the contrary, it adheres to the fundamental belief of modern society that there must be ever more worldly goods to be enjoyed, the spoils of a conquest of nature which is held to be man's noblest venture. The socialist ideal is grafted on to the progressive society and adheres to this society's veneration of commodities, its encouragement of fleshly appetites and pride in technical imperialism.

The moral seduction of socialism lies in the fact that it repudiates the methodical exploitation of the personal interest motive, of the fleshly appetites, of egoism, which held pride of place in the economic society it has undertaken to supersede; yet that, insofar as it has endorsed this society's pursuit of ever-increasing consumption, it has become a heterogeneous system, torn by an inner contradiction.

If "more goods" are the goal to which society's efforts are to be addressed, why should "more goods" be a disreputable objective for the individual? Socialism suffers from ambiguity in its judgment of values: If the good of society lies in greater riches, why not the good of the individual? If society should press toward that good, why not the individual? If this appetite for riches is wrong in the individual, why not in society? Here, then, is at least a *prima facie* incoherence, indeed a blatant heterogeneity.

Further, so long as the general purpose of society is the conquest of nature and the enjoyment of its spoils, is it not logical that this purpose should determine the characteristics of that society? Is not society shaped by its predominant desire, by the end toward which it tends? Is it not possible that many unpleasant traits of society are functionally related to its basic purpose? And is not their unpleasantness inherent in the purpose, so that any different society one seeks to build up with the same purpose must display the same characteristics, possibly under a different guise?

The productivist society may be likened to the military society. That which is meant for war must in its structure show characteristics appropriate to war. An army, or a military society, embodies many traits which are indefensible by the standards of a "good society." But military hierarchy and discipline cannot be done away with as long as victory remains the purpose—though of course they can be amended. In the same manner, there may be a relation between the structure of productivist society and its purpose. And there is much to be said for the view that socialism's higher aspirations were doomed when it accepted the general purpose of modern society —as Rousseau indeed foresaw.

The socialist belief, that is to say the noble ethical aim of society rid of its antagonisms and transformed into a city of brotherly love, has gone into decline. The measures which were once believed to lead toward that goal are still pressed for and in no small degree achieved. But they are increasingly advocated as ends, or as means to something other than the "good society" previously pictured, the vision of which now floats free from its anchor to what was formerly believed to be its means of achievement. Socialism, properly so called, is disintegrating, in that the component parts of a formerly compact edifice of beliefs seem to be operating almost autonomously and for something differing from the original socialist ideal.

This would please Sorel or Pareto, as an illustration of their theories of myths.

Redistribution and the scandal of poverty

What has now come to the fore, as against the ideal of fair rewards and brotherly love, is the ideal of more equal consumption. It may be regarded as compounded of two convictions: *one*, that it is good and necessary to remove want and that the surplus of some should be sacrificed to the urgent needs of others; and *two*, that inequality of means between the several members of a society is bad in itself and should be more or less radically removed.

The two ideas are not logically related. The first rests squarely upon the Christian idea of brotherhood. Man is his brother's keeper, must act as the Good Samaritan, has a moral obligation to help the unfortunate, an obligation that rests most heavily, though not exclusively, upon the most fortunate.[12] There is, on the other hand, no *prima facie* evidence for the current contention that justice demands near equality of material conditions. Justice means proportion. The individualist is entitled to hold that justice demands individual rewards proportionate to individual endeavors; and the socialist is entitled to hold that it demands individual rewards proportionate to the services received by the community.[13] It seems therefore reasonable to deny simultaneously that our present society

[12] Christ's bidding to the rich is most imperative. Is it necessary to stress that while he urged the rich young man to "distribute unto the poor," he did not tell the poor to take upon themselves to distribute by taxation the rich young man's wealth. While the moral value of the first process is evident, that of the second is not.

[13] The socialist alluded to in this place is not the "utopian" socialist mainly preoccupied with the brotherhood of man, but the "organic" socialist who reasons in terms of the society as a whole.

is just and that justice is to be achieved by the equalization of incomes.

It is, however, a loose modern habit to call "just" whatever is thought emotionally desirable. Attention was legitimately called in the nineteenth century to the sorry condition of the laboring classes. It was felt to be wrong that their human needs were so ill-satisfied. The idea of proportion then came to be applied to the relation between needs and resources. Just as it seemed improper that some should have less than what was adjudged necessary, so it also seemed improper that others should have so much more.

The first feeling was almost the only one at work in the early stage of redistributionism. The second has almost gained the upper hand in the latter stage.[14]

Socialists, at the inception of the move toward redistribution, took rather a disdainful attitude; the initial measures were in their eyes mere bribes offered to the working classes in an attempt to divert them from the higher aims of socialism.

Here, however, powerful feelings were aroused. While it is difficult for men to imagine the suppression of private property, that is, of something that all desire, it is natural to them to compare their condition with that of others; the poorer can easily imagine the uses to which they would put some of the riches of others, and the richer, if once awakened to the condition of the poorer, are bound to feel some remorse on account of their luxuries.

At all times the revelation of poverty has come as a shock to the chosen few: It has impelled them to regard their personal extravagance with a sense of guilt, has

---

[14] Indeed, there are some redistributionists who would be less satisfied by a lifting up of the whole scale of incomes, preserving their present inequality, than by a flattening down of the inequalities.

driven them to distribute their riches and to mingle with the poor. In every case one knows of in the past, this has been associated with a religious experience: The mind may have been turned to God by the discovery of the poor, or to the poor by the discovery of God; in any case the two are linked, and a revulsion away from riches as evil was always implied.

However, in our century the feeling that has assailed not merely a few spirits but practically all the members of the leading classes has been of a different kind. Upon a society inordinately proud of its ever-increasing riches dawned that "in the midst of plenty," as the saying went, misery was still rife; and this called for action to raise the standard of the poor. While the discovery of poverty, coupled with an assumption of the impossibility of removing it, had formerly brought about a revulsion against riches, this time a deep-rooted appreciation of worldly goods, coupled with a sense of power, caused an onslaught on poverty itself. Riches had been a scandal in the face of poverty; now poverty was a scandal in the face of riches. (Compare with modern statements[15] the previous identification of poverty with holiness.) To the pace-making middle classes, profoundly committed to the religion of progress, the existence of poverty was not only emotionally but intellectually disturbing, in the same manner as is the existence of evil to the simpler sort of deist. The increasing goodness of civilization, the increasing power of man, were to be finally demonstrated by the eradication of poverty.

Thus, charity and pride went hand in hand. In stressing the role played by pride, it is not intended to belittle the part given to charity. Assuredly there are moments in history when the human heart is suddenly mel-

---

[15] Cf. Bernard Shaw: "I hate the poor."

lowed and some phenomenon of this kind occurs. Thus, redistribution was sped on its way by a feeling, or pattern of feelings. How this feeling came to be operative at a given moment is a problem for historians and is not germane to our topic.

The notions of relief and of lifting working-class standards merged

We must, however, note that redistribution appears as a novelty only in contrast to the practices immediately preceding it and in the choice of its agent, the State. It is inherent in the very notion of society that those in direct want must be taken care of. The principle is applied in every family and in every small community, and in fact went out of practice only a few generations ago as a result of the disruption of smaller communities by the Industrial Revolution. This caused the isolation of the individual, and the new "master" he acquired did not regard himself as bound to him by the same tie as the former lord. It is characteristic that the feasts of consumption of the landed class were feasts *for all*, whereas the consumption of the rich in the new era is purely selfish. It is, moreover, almost needless to point out that the Church, when it enjoyed enormous gifts from the powerful and the rich, was a great redistributive agency. Between the old customs and the age of the welfare state stretch the "hard times," when the individual was left helpless in his need.

This cannot be ascribed to lack of feeling in generations which were fired with sympathy for slaves, for oppressed nationalities, and with indignation at the news of the "Bulgarian atrocities." One is tempted to conclude that men's powers of sympathy vary in their direction over periods of time and are somewhat limited at any one moment. However, concern for the least favored was certainly not absent, as Malthus, Sismondi, and many others testify.

The twentieth century offers no more forceful statement of maldistribution than that of John Stuart Mill.[16] But it was assumed that the standard of life of "the people" would be raised by the cheapening of goods, of which the cheapening of salt and spices offered a promising instance.[17] Moreover, the relative position of the laborer would be improved by the cheapening of capital. Faith in the benefits of a competitive economy for "the

[16] "If therefore the choice were to be between Communism with all its chances and the present (1852) state of society with all its sufferings and injustices; if the institution of private property necessarily carried with it as a consequence that the produce of labour should be apportioned as we now see it, almost in an inverse ratio to the labour; the largest proportions to those who have never worked at all, the next largest to those whose work is purely nominal, and so in a descending scale, the remuneration dwindling as the work grows harder and more disagreeable, until the most fatiguing and exhausting bodily labour cannot count with certainty on being able to earn even the necessaries of life; if this or Communism were the alternative, all the difficulties, great or small, of Communism would be as dust in the balance." Mill, *Principles of Political Economy*, II, i, par. 3.

[17] "There are some things the current prices of which in this country are very low even to the poorer classes; such as, for instance, salt, and many kinds of savours and spices, and also cheap medicines. It is doubtful whether any fall in price would induce a considerable increase in the consumption of these." Marshall, *Principles*, III, iv, 3. These very things had once been luxuries. Therefore, it was not unreasonable to hope that other commodities would successively fall from the category of those whose consumption is elastic to the category of inelastic consumption, of goods cheap enough for any decrease in price to fail to cause a rise in consumption. Marshall cited the case of sugar, which had previously belonged to the class of elastic consumption: "A little while ago sugar belonged in this group of commodities; but its price in England has fallen so far as to be low relatively even to the working classes and the demand for it, therefore, is not elastic."

common man" was not ill-grounded, as the American example testifies. But perhaps there was some confusion between two different notions: *one*, that the situation of the "median" worker is best improved by the play of productive forces; and *two*, that there is no call to take care of an unfortunate "rearguard." Such is the "stickiness" of social thinking that as long as emphasis was laid on the raising of the median by the processes of the market, there was reluctance to intervene on behalf of the unfortunate (compare the attitude of the American Federation of Labor in the first years of the Great Depression), while as soon as attention was focused upon this rearguard, it came to be held that the median condition was also to be raised by political measures.

While relief is an unquestionable social obligation which the destruction of neighborliness, of responsible aristocracies, and of Church wealth has laid on the State for want of any other agency, it is open to discussion whether policies of redistribution are the best means of dealing with the problem of raising *median* working incomes, whether they can be effective, and whether they do not come into conflict with other legitimate social objectives.

The distinction drawn here is admittedly a difficult one. The two things are confused in practice, and it is not always clear to which end the enormous social machinery set up in our generation is actually working; this creation of ours presents a structure not easily amenable to our intellectual categories. When, through the working of the social services, a man in actual want is provided with the means of subsistence, whether it be a minimum income in days of unemployment or basic medical care for which he could not have paid, this is a primary manifestation of solidarity. And it does not come under redistribution as we understand it here.

What does come under redistribution is everything which relieves the individual of an expenditure that he could and presumably would have undertaken out of his own purse, and which, freeing a proportion of his income, is therefore equivalent to a raising of this income. A family which would have bought the same amount of food at non-subsidized prices and gets it so much cheaper, an individual who would have sought the same medical services and gets them free, see their incomes raised. And this is what we want to discuss.

As we know, this does not apply only to poorer people: In some countries, especially in England, all incomes are raised in this manner while most incomes are drawn upon to finance the raising. The impact upon incomes of this enormous diversion and redistribution is a very complicated subject with which we are not ready to deal. It is far from being a simple redistribution from the richer to the poorer. And yet it is to a large degree sustained by a belief in the rightness of redistribution from the richer to the poorer and by the belief that this is what the whole process comes to. This basic motivating thought is what we want to deal with.

Indecent low-living and indecent high-living

We propose to deal with redistribution in its pure form; that is, taking from the higher incomes to add to the lower incomes. Such a policy is sustained by a pattern of feelings from which we shall try to extract some implied judgments of value. The urge to redistribute is closely attended by a sense of scandal: It is scandalous that so many should be in dire need, and it is also scandalous that so many more should have an inadequate mode of life, which seems to us, in the original sense of the word, indecent. Thus, the urge to redistribute is associated more or less with an idea of a *floor* beneath which no one should be left.

In thinking of the higher incomes, we are also conscious of an indecency: The upper modes of life seem to us wasteful of riches which could cover far more legitimate needs. That is, if you will, condemnation by comparison. But there is, moreover, a certain "way of the rich" which seems to us to call for absolute condemnation. We should in any event have scant sympathy with expenditure in night clubs, casinos, on horse-racing and so on.

These two judgments of value are generally fused in the very general feeling which may be termed the "caviar into bread" motive. Not only do we disapprove of the feast of caviar when others lack bread but we disapprove of it absolutely. Therefore, when these two feelings are involved, of comparative disapproval and absolute disapproval, no hesitation is felt in pronouncing that the transfer of such surplus is desirable.[18] These illustrations of "silly" expenditure are always uppermost in minds contemplating redistribution.

But of course such judgments upon proper levels of consumption, which we have called "absolute," are relative to a certain society at a certain time. They are in fact the subjective judgments of the policy-making class—in our times of the lower-middle class. In fact the levels of

[18] The idea, mentioned in our quotation of Mill, that the higher incomes are probably undeserved is also operative. It is, of course, related to the aforementioned principle of fair reward. But we do not have to take it into account here, since the policies of redistribution make little use of it. The difference in treatment between earned and unearned incomes is slight; nor is any made according to the means of earning incomes—no more is allowed to the creator than to the man whose activity is purely repetitive or even whose "earnings" are drawn from a monopoly situation.

consumption which it deems the suitable minimum and the acceptable maximum are projections of its tastes. It is class that forms social opinion which also makes up the social standards for what is indecent high-living and indecent low-living.[19]

The floor and the ceiling: Intellectual harmony and financial harmony

We now need a terminology which we shall keep within modest bounds. We call *floor* the minimum income regarded as necessary and *ceiling* the maximum income regarded as desirable. We call floor and ceiling "intellectually harmonious" insofar as they are the floor and ceiling acceptable to the same mind or minds. Further, we shall call a floor and ceiling "financially harmonious" insofar as there is sufficient surplus to be taken from "above the ceiling" incomes to make up the deficiency in "beneath the floor" incomes. Thus, if a is the floor and there are A incomes beneath it which fall short of Aa by the sum L, the ceiling h is financially harmonious with the floor a if the incomes of the class H (the people who have incomes greater than h) are equal or superior to $Hh + L$.

If, on the other hand, a and h are an intellectually harmonious set of floor-and-ceiling and the incomes of the H people who enjoy more than h are $Hh + S$ and S falls short of L, then a and h are not financially harmonious.

Redistributionism is a spontaneous feeling. And in its more naïve forms it carries with it an implied conviction that the floor and ceiling which are intellectually harmo-

---

[19] It is well known that "the people" are less critical of high-living than the *petite bourgeoisie*. When this high-living has a spectacular value, as in the case of aristocracy, or today in the case of film actors and similar public figures, there is great tolerance of it among "the people."

nious will also prove to be financially harmonious. This, like so many spontaneous assumptions of the human mind, is an error. Questioning members of the western intelligentsia, unfamiliar with income statistics, on the suitable floor and ceiling of incomes, is absorbingly interesting. They always set a and h much too high for financial harmony. The surplus S always falls very far short of the deficiency L to be made up.

This error is encouraged by a nodding acquaintance with income distribution statistics. Any income statistics can show that a large percentage of total personal income is held by a small percentage of recipients. Such statistics were persuasively advanced in the United States during the New Deal. This technique can be applied to British incomes, and here again the results are impressive. Taking incomes *before taxation*, 3.14% of income holders enjoy 19.4% of the personal incomes; 5.16% enjoy 24.5% of the incomes; and finally 12% enjoy 36.3% of the incomes. Such grouping of incomes seems to afford enormous possibilities for redistribution. But it is to be stressed that our first class comprises all income holders down to £1000 gross, the second down to £750, and the third down to £500.[20]

Few would put the ceiling as low as a thousand pounds gross,[21] thus putting the maximum net earned income of a single person at £700 15s. and that of a family with three children at £813 5s. But, should one agree to

---

[20] Many of those who denounce the disproportionate share of the "upper tenth" are blissfully unconscious of belonging to it.

[21] Thus maximum net income would be:

	(if all earned income)	(if all investment income)
for a single person	£700 15s.	£625 15s.
for a childless couple	£732 5s.	£657 5s.
for a couple with three children	£813 5s.	£738 5s.

do so, the sums available for redistribution would be far less than it would seem at first sight. From the total amount of incomes above the ceiling, the income allowed would first have to be subtracted; second, unless one were prepared to restrict the functions of the State, the Treasury would have to recoup itself for its losses resulting from this redistribution. While it obtains £612 millions in direct taxation from incomes above £1000, it could hope to take from the sum redistributed to nether incomes only a negligible fraction of the former amount. It would then have to subtract from this sum the difference between its present takings and its takings under the new allotment of incomes, or alternatively raise very considerably the rate of taxation on nether incomes. It is easiest to picture this problem as met by a deduction in favor of the exchequer from the amount available for redistribution. Nor is this deduction the last one; if it is proposed to maintain the level of national investment, the difference between the amount of savings at present contributed by the higher incomes and the savings to be expected from the same amount in new hands must again be deducted. The amount finally found to be transferable bears little relation to the hopes evoked.

How low a ceiling?

In an Appendix we have attempted to calculate how a given floor of incomes could be obtained by lopping off the tops of all incomes above a certain ceiling. In this treatment, the ceiling is the unknown quantity. The result of our calculations is a ceiling far beneath any *a priori* estimate. In order to achieve our floor, we cannot be content to remove the surplus of the rich; we must eat deeply into lower-middle-class incomes. A maximum net income of £500 is something no champion of redistribution has contemplated, yet that is what we arrive at. Incidentally, our calculations bring out the neglected fact that the present degree of redistribution would aready be impracticable were it, as one believes, essentially a redistribution from the rich to the poor; it proves possible because it is quite as much a horizontal shift as an oblique drift.

The outcome of this exploration comes as something of a surprise. It jolts a widely held belief that our societies are extremely rich and that their wealth is merely maldistributed—a belief unwisely disseminated by the well-meaning abundance-mongers of the thirties. What we do find is that such surpluses as we might be willing ruthlessly to take away—always assuming that this would have no effect upon production—are by a long way inadequate to raise our nether incomes to a desirable level. The pursuit of our purpose involves the debasement of even the lower-middle-class standard of life.

Redistributionism was at the outset given its impetus by two absolute disapprovals; the unrightness of underconsumption was matched by the unrightness of overconsumption. What luck if, in order to achieve a worthy purpose, you have to sacrifice nothing of value, if indeed your means to the suppression of an evil are also desirable of themselves! Thus the problem appeared to the intellectual, sitting in judgment upon society. There were bad patterns of life, those of the poor, which he wished to do away with; and he expected that this could be accomplished merely by the suppression of other bad patterns of life, those of the rich. The intellectual (not the artist) is naturally out of sympathy with the extrovert way of life of the rich. There was thus no social loss, in his eyes, implied in redistribution policies. But if the income ceiling is to be brought as low as we have suggested, then there is a great change. It is now worthy patterns of life which are to be destroyed, standards which the intellectual has been accustomed to and which he holds necessary to the performance of those social functions he most appreciates.

And so, while it still seems right to give, the rightness of taking away is far less obvious. It is easy to say: "Rothschild must forgo his yacht." It is quite another thing to say: "I am afraid Bergson must lose the modest competence which made it possible for him to do his work." Nor is it only a question of unearned income: The executive, the public servant, the engineer, the intellectual, the artist are to be cramped. Is this desirable? Is this right?

There is ample evidence that it is not regarded as desirable or right by the most extreme champions of redistribution. For the remunerations attached to the ever-multiplying functions of the redistributing State are far above the ceilings which result from our investigation. No more positive proof could be adduced that such ceilings are not in fact regarded as desirable or acceptable by the advocates of redistribution. Owing, however, to the fallibility of man, it is quite possible that redistributionists are right in advocating redistribution and wrong in providing relatively high incomes for its agents. This may be a concession to surrounding circumstances, a carry-over of inherited notions, an inconsistency. Let us therefore examine without prejudice the possibility that sacrifices from even modest incomes may be justified in order to supplement our minus incomes.

As we now have to weigh the disadvantages of an abnormally low middle-class ceiling as against that of still insufficient working-class incomes, we must seek some criterion of rightness. We are offered the "arithmetic of happiness," the felicific calculus, now coated over with new paint as the economics of welfare.

A discussion of satisfactions

Redistribution started with a feeling that some have too
little and some too much. When attempts are made to ex-
press this feeling more precisely, two formulae are spontaneously offered. The first we may call objective, the
second subjective. The objective formula is based upon
an idea of a decent way of life beneath which no one
should fall and above which other ways of life are desirable and acceptable within a certain range. The subjective
formula is not based upon a notion of what is objectively
good for men but can be roughly stated as follows: "The
richer would feel their loss less than the poorer would
appreciate their gain"; or even more roughly: "A certain
loss of income would mean less to the richer than the
consequent gain would mean to the poorer."

Here a comparison of satisfactions is made. Can such a
comparison be rendered effective? Can we with any pre-
cision come to weigh losses of satisfaction to some and
gains of satisfaction to others? If so, we may know how
to achieve the maximum sum of individual satisfactions
capable of being drawn from a given flow of production,
which must always be assumed to be unaffected.

Such an idea was bound to arise in the circle of economists. For maximization of satisfactions in various con-
texts has been for several generations a familiar notion.
In the pure theory of consumer's demand, the individual
is conceived of as provided with a given income which he
allots among the various goods offered by the market at
given prices, in such a way as to give himself maximum
satisfaction. The pure theory of exchange deals with two
parties, each provided with a supply of a certain commodity, each desiring the commodity held by the other.
Each barters away *quanta* of the good held against *quanta*
of the good desired until any further acquisition involves

a greater sacrifice than the acquisition is worth to him. In that position, each can be said to have achieved the collection most satisfactory to him—in a certain sense, the satisfaction of both is maximized.[22] The somewhat mythical concept of general equilibrium carries this further to the case of many people and many commodities. General equilibrium is an aesthetic and mathematical optimum which economists have been prone to equate, either expressly or by implication, with an optimum of satisfactions. This was indeed an intuitive necessity for economists. Postulating that economic behavior is ruled by the effort to maximize individual satisfactions, deducing that any equilibrium in exchange is the happiest compromise between the satisfactions of the parties and thus somehow maximizes the sum of their satisfactions, they were led to regard general equilibrium as the best the individual can do for himself as against all others, and, from a bird's eye view, as the best possible combination of individual results.[23] Now, as soon as one adopts this idea of the best possible combination, it follows logically that any departure from general equilibrium involves a balance of increased dissatisfactions over increased satisfactions. Thus, as soon as one attaches any psychological connotation to general equilibrium, one is involved in comparing the satisfactions of different individuals, or at least their differentials.

Now, obviously, general equilibrium involves for each individual a certain optimum, relative only to his given means, and general equilibrium as a whole will be different according to differences in the initial distribution of

[22] See Prof. Nogaro's discussion in *La Valeur Logique des Théories Economiques* (Paris, 1947), chap. IX, "La Théorie du Maximum de Satisfactions."

[23] See Samuelson's discussion in *Foundations of Economic Analysis* (Cambridge, 5 March 1948), chap. VIII, "Economy of Welfare."

incomes. If general equilibrium is to be comparable, for the superiority of all-round satisfaction that it involves, with a less-than-equilibrium situation, then also a general equilibrium pursuant to a certain initial distribution must be held comparable to another general equilibrium arising from another initial distribution. Thus, the very notion of general equilibrium as a position from which any departure involves a net loss of satisfactions leads directly into welfare economics, and in fact provides them with their blatantly Paretian definitions.

The theory of diminishing utility

Not only has maximization of satisfactions played a ruling part in modern economics as developed by Walras and Jevons, but the great tool of generations of economists since the days of these pioneers has been the axiom of diminishing utility. The fact that a given fraction of good a is the less valuable to the holder the more he holds of good a beautifully explains the gain both parties achieve in exchange, each abandoning "last" fractions of that which he has most of in order to gain "first" fractions of that which he has not got. Two sets of goods a and b, at first collected each in one hand, gain in value by the operation of exchange since last fractions of a, of little utility to A, pass into the hands of B, to whom they are more useful, while A acquires B's last fractions of b, which are more valuable to him than to their previous holder.

Two things are to be considered in this operation of exchange. As he abandons his last fraction of a, the holder A loses little, and as he acquires his first fraction of b, he acquires much. Supposing him now so amply provided with $b, c \ldots n$, that he is not tempted to acquire fractions of *b*, still the abandonment of the last fraction of *a* is but a small sacrifice. Moreover, for B the acquisition of the first fraction of *a* is a great gain; this fraction of *a* by changing hands can still be said to be gaining value in use.

This constitutes the transition from the axiom of diminishing utility to the assumption of diminishing utility of income.

Outstanding economists have found no difficulty in extending the axiom of diminishing utility to income. Thus Professor Pigou: "It is evident that any transference of income from a relatively rich man to a relatively poor man of similar temperament, since it enables more intense wants to be satisfied at the expense of less intense wants, must increase the aggregate sum of satisfactions."[24] This statement, by virtue of its informality, is more readily accepted than Professor Lerner's imposing: "Total satisfaction is maximized by that division of incomes which equalizes the marginal utilities of income of all the individuals in the society."[25]

Marginal utility of income is really a fancy name for the satisfaction or pleasure derived from the last unit of income. Let this be £10. Professor Lerner's statement means that income is well distributed when the loss of £10 would cause the same discomfort to any member of the society. Professor Pigou's statement means that the shift of £10 from one individual to another is justified as long as in new hands the £10 will yield more satisfaction than in the former.

Professor Robbins has argued,[26] with his usual elegance, that the stretching of diminishing marginal utility to income is unwarranted, that marginalism in this field

[24] Pigou, *Economics of Welfare*, 4th ed. (London, 1948), p. 89.

[25] A. P. Lerner, *The Economics of Control*, 3rd ed. (1947), chap. II, p. 29.

[26] Lionel Robbins, *An Essay on the Nature and Significance of Economic Science*, 2nd ed. (London, 1935), chap. VI.

involves a comparison of the satisfactions of different persons and thus falls into the very trap that in its legitimate applications it had sought to avoid. Satisfactions of different persons cannot, he says, be measured with a common rod.

This argument, however, turns out a boon in disguise to the welfarist who had saddled himself with the impossible task of equating the marginal utilities of different individuals. By proving this a stalemate, Professor Robbins unwillingly induces a new move: "The probable value of total satisfactions is maximized by dividing income *evenly*" (Lerner).[27] It is not necessary to dwell upon Professor Lerner's demonstration, which rests upon the highly artificial assumptions that the initial condition is one of equality and that moves away from it are haphazard. The strength of the case for even distribution does not lie in this formal reasoning. It lies in that, as soon as equal distribution is proposed as the solution to the maximization of satisfactions, those who oppose it have laid upon themselves the burden of proving that those who in fact draw the greater incomes have the greater capacity for enjoyment—an undertaking in which they cannot fail to shock every presupposition of a democratic society.

Further points and qualifications

Therefore, in a discussion of the maximization of satisfactions, however the ball is set rolling, it must come to rest on the solution of even distribution. That, however, is on the assumption that the holders of incomes have not developed their lives and tastes in accordance with their in-

[27] Lerner, *The Economics of Control*, pp. 29–32.

comes, a qualification rightly stressed by Professor Pigou.[28]

It must be granted that a loss of income is a loss of definite satisfactions, while a gain of income beyond a certain proportion is a gain of as yet indefinite satisfactions. What is far more important, the marginalist representation of income as a progression of diminishing terms, the last of which can always be severed without affecting the others, does not hold good all along the line. A certain way of life implies a certain layout of expenditures out of which some "water" can always be "wrung." But when a certain point is reached, the same way of life cannot be maintained; a major readjustment is necessary; there is a fall to another way of life, a fall which involves great dissatisfaction.

Therefore, it can be held that the previous discussion of satisfactions failed to do justice to the intensity of dissatisfactions due to loss of income. As we are still ruled by Robbins' principle that satisfactions and dissatisfactions of different persons are not commensurable, one falls back upon the mode of measurement which effectively prevails. It is not to be proven that the sum of individual satisfactions of people benefited is greater than the sum of dissatisfactions of people despoiled. In fact there is every reason to believe that if what is taken from a number of people were distributed among an equal number of people, the latter would gain less total satisfaction than the former were losing. But the fact is that the takings are distributed among a far greater number of people. And there will be more people pleased than displeased, more positive signs than negative; and as the intensity of the values is not to be measured, all one can do is state that there are more positive signs than negative

[28] Pigou, *A Study in Public Finance*, 3rd ed. (London, 1947), p. 90.

and take the result as a gain, which is what in fact is currently done.

It is, however, generally granted that the intensity of dissatisfactions should not be pushed too far, and the process of reducing upper incomes is therefore to be effected over a period of time.

It has been suggested that the assumed impossibility of measuring dissatisfactions against satisfactions might be overcome by empirical means. If indeed we took Lansing's view of democracy as a regime of well-regulated strife where force is made to prevail without violence, we might say that the dissatisfaction caused by loss of income is measured by the political resistance opposed to measures of redistribution, and that success or failure of this resistance denotes the excess of dissatisfaction over satisfaction or the contrary. Thus, the outcome of the political struggle over incomes would always maximize welfare.

However, it would be so only if all protagonists were concerned with nothing but their personal satisfaction and were indifferent to any moral imperative. Then indeed the vigor of their several demands would be expressive of the intensity of their satisfactions. Fortunately, the struggle occurs nowhere in such a climate of clear and conscious selfishness.

Discrimination against minorities

The inexpediency of radical leveling in the short run is easily granted. The psychologist warns of the violent, socially disruptive discontent of those suddenly toppled down from their customary modes of life.[29] The econo-

---

[29] The remarkable consent of the British higher-income classes to a sharp fall in economic status was got from their patriotism, during a

mist warns that the conversion to popular use of those productive resources which specifically served the well-to-do will not, in the short run, yield in popular goods and services anything like the value previously yielded in luxury goods and services.[30]

Conceding objections to short-run leveling does not weaken the case for long-run leveling. Indeed it strengthens it. For the greater willingness one shows to postpone radical equalization in order to accommodate acquired tastes, the more one implies that differences in subjective wants are a matter of habit, a historic phenomenon. While it would seem excessive to equalize incomes between the men of today, known to us and whom we know to have different needs, it seems plausible to do so

war which threatened national existence. The "silent revolution" was really achieved by a war-waging national government. Whether so rapid a descent would have been accepted as willingly in peace, for an avowed purpose of social redistribution, is a matter for doubt. It might then have bred an upper-class resentment which tends to weaken a commonwealth.

[30] Professor Devons lends me this formulation: "It might be quite a long time before the facilities which are used to provide expensive commodities could in fact be redirected profitably to alternative uses."

I had originally thought that the loss of outlet for the expensive commodities, resulting from radical redistribution, implied more than merely a friction phenomenon; that services, worth a million pounds to the rich, could not, when redirected to the poor, be worth anything like the same amount. This intuitive belief was based largely upon the fact that the rich pay each other fancy prices for their services, as between a fashionable doctor and a fashionable lawyer, thus generating an inner circuit of inflated values which must flicker out of existence with the suppression of the higher incomes. The very existence of these incomes causes a high-pricing of skills which both adds to these incomes and absorbs part of their expenditure. It seems to me that all this would suffer a deflation under radical redistribution and that therefore the buying power transferred would suffer some shrinkage in the process.

But both Dr. Ronald F. Henderson and Professor Devons have kindly taken the trouble to refuse my view on sound theoretical grounds, and I bow to their judgment.

in the case of men whose personalities we can imagine to differ less from one another—for the very good reason that they have as yet no personalities. Thereby we can project forward as reasonable what might in reality strike us as absurd.

It is a common behavior of the mind, naturally enamored of simplicity, to build its schemes far away from the annoying complexities of a familiar reality, in the future or in a mythical past, where things have no shapes of their own. After this first operation resulting in a rational scheme, that scheme can be used as a rational model against which the disorderly architecture of today can be measured and thereby condemned.

Let us, however, notice a certain consequence of equalization, valid in whatever future we care to place the completion of reform. Let us grant that any differences in tastes due to social habits have been erased. Men will not, however, be uniform in character; some differences in tastes must exist among individuals. Economic demand will not any more be weighted by differences in individual incomes that will have been abolished: It will be weighted solely by numbers. It is clear that those goods and services in demand by greater collections of individuals will be provided to those individuals more cheaply than other goods and services wanted by smaller collections of individuals will be provided to these latter. The satisfaction of minority wants will be more expensive than the satisfaction of majority wants. Members of a minority will be discriminated against.

There is nothing novel in this phenomenon. It is a regular feature of any economic society. People of uncommon tastes are at a disadvantage for the satisfaction of their wants. But they can and do endeavor to raise their incomes in order to pay for their distinctive wants. And this, by the way, is a most potent incentive; its efficiency is illustrated by the more than average effort, the higher incomes and the leading positions achieved by racial and religious minorities; what is true of these well-defined minorities is just as true of individuals presenting original traits. Sociologists will readily grant that, in a society where free competition obtains, the more active and the more successful are also those with the more uncommon personalities.

If, however, it is not open to those whose tastes differ from the common run to remedy their economic disadvantage by an increase in their incomes, then, in the name of equality, they will be enduring discrimination.[31]

Four consequences deserve notice. First, personal hardship for individuals of original tastes; second, the loss to society of the special effort these people would make in order to satisfy their special needs; third, the loss to society of the variety in ways of life resulting from successful efforts to satisfy special wants; fourth, the loss to society of those activities which are supported by minority demands.

With respect to the latter point, it is a commonplace that things which are now provided inexpensively to the many, say spices or the newspaper, were originally luxuries which could be offered only because some few were willing and able to buy them at high prices. It is difficult to say what the economic development of the West

---

[31] Reading offers a minor but clear instance of the discrimination referred to. Say that the Primus household acquires every month twelve books of the shilling kind: The total cost is 12s. The Secundus household has different tastes which run to less popular books, costing from 7s. 6d. to 21s. If the Secundus household is to have the same amount of reading matter, it may have to spend something like £6: ten times as much as the Primus household. This means, if incomes are equal, that in fact the Secundus household will be at a disadvantage for the satisfaction of its other needs (without having a greater quantity of reading matter).

would have been, had first things been put first, as reformers urge; that is, if the productive effort had been
aimed at providing more of the things needed by all, to
the exclusion of a greater variety of things desired by minorities. But the onus of proving that economic progress
would have been as impressive surely rests with the reformers. History shows us that each successive enlargement of the opportunities to consume was linked with
unequal distribution of means to consume.[32]

The effect of redistribution upon society

No one has attempted to draw the picture of the society
which would result from radical redistribution, as called
for by the logic of reasoning on the maximization of satisfactions. Even if one were to compromise on such a floor-
and-ceiling society as we attempt to work out in the Appendix, it would still be one which would exclude the
present modes of life of our leaders in every field,
whether they are businessmen, public servants, artists,
intellectuals, or trade-unionists.

We have forbidden ourselves to contemplate any decrease in the activity of anyone, any lowering of production as a whole. But the reallocation of incomes would
bring about a great shift in activities. The demand for
some goods and services would be increased. The de-

---

[32] In recent years, public opinion has been made increasingly aware of
the part played by the accumulation of capital in economic progress.
No attention has yet been paid to the relationship between the distribution of buying power and progress. Experience shows that progress is discouraged where inequality is excessive, hereditary, and
where the scale of incomes is discontinuous. But also that it is discouraged where equality is enforced. There may be an optimal allocation of consuming power for the purposes of progress. The subject
might be worth exploring.

mand for others would drop or disappear. It is not beyond the skill of those economists who have specialized in consumer behavior to calculate roughly how far the demand of certain items would rise and how far the demand of certain others would drop.[33]

A number of the present activities of our society would fade out for lack of a buyer. Thereby Wicksteed's "misdirection of productive activities" would be redressed. This great economist argued with feeling that inequality of income distorts the allocation of productive resources;[34] efforts in a free market economy being directed to the point at which they will be best remunerated, the rich can draw such efforts away from the satisfaction of poor men's urgent wants to the satisfaction of rich men's whims. The big incomes are, so to speak, magnets attracting efforts away from their best application. In our reformed society, this evil would be done away with.

I for one would see without chagrin the disappearance of many activities which serve the richer, but no one surely would gladly accept the disappearance of all the activities which find their market in the classes enjoying more than £500 of net income. The production of all first-quality goods would cease. The skill they demand would be lost and the taste they shape would be coarsened. The production of artistic and intellectual goods would be af-

---

[33] In the case of the upward movement of lower incomes, the use of additional financial means can be predicted with a high degree of certainty. The change for individual families would remain well within the range of changes which do occur in present social conditions, the results of which are well known. The downward movement of upper incomes, on the other hand, would be for individual families a very radical change, of which we have in our society too few examples from which to generalize. Reasonable surmises can, however, be made.

[34] P.H. Wicksteed, *Common Sense in Political Economy* (London, 1933), pp. 189–91.

fected first and foremost. Who could buy paintings? Who even could buy books other than pulp?

Can we reconcile ourselves to the loss suffered by civilization if creative intellectual and artistic activities fail to find a market? We must if we follow the logic of the felicific calculus. If the 2,000 guineas heretofore spent by 2,000 buyers of an original piece of historical or philosophical research are henceforth spent by 42,000 buyers of shilling books, aggregate satisfaction is very probably enhanced. There is therefore a gain to society, according to this mode of thought which represents society as a collection of independent consumers. Felicific calculus, counting in units of satisfactions afforded to individuals, cannot enter into its accounts the loss involved in the suppression of the piece of research—a fact which, by the way, brings to light the radically individualistic assumptions of a viewpoint usually labeled socialistic.

In fact, and although this entails an intellectual inconsistency, the most eager champions of income redistribution are highly sensitive to the cultural losses involved. And they press upon us a strong restorative. It is true that individuals will not be able to build up private libraries; but there will be bigger and better and ever more numerous public libraries. It is true that the producer of the book will not be sustained by individual buyers; but the author will be given a public grant, and so forth. All advocates of extreme redistribution couple it with most generous measures of state support for the whole superstructure of cultural activities. This calls for two comments. We shall deal first with the measures of compensation and then with their significance.

The more redistribution, the more power to the State

Already, when stressing the loss of investment capital which would result from a redistribution of incomes, we found that the necessary counterpart of lopping off the tops of higher incomes was the diversion by the State from these incomes of as much, or almost as much, as they used to pour into investment; the assumption which followed logically was that the State would take care of investment: a great function, a great responsibility, and a great power.

Now we find that by making it impossible for individuals to support cultural activities out of their shrunken incomes, we have developed upon the State another great function, another great power.

It then follows that the State finances, and therefore chooses, investments; and that it finances cultural activities and must thenceforth choose which it supports. There being no private buyers left for books or paintings or other creative work, the State must support literature and the arts either as buyer or as provider of *beneficia* to the producers, or in both capacities.

This is a rather disquieting thought. How quickly this State mastery follows upon measures of redistribution we can judge by the enormous progress toward such mastery which has already followed from limited redistribution.

Values and satisfactions

But the fact that redistributionists are eager to repair by State expenditure the degradation of higher activities which would result from redistribution left to itself is very significant. They want to prevent a loss of values.

Does this make sense? In the whole process of reasoning which sought to justify redistribution rationally, it was assumed that the individual's satisfaction was to be maximized and that the maximization of the sum of individual satisfactions was to be sought. It was granted for argument's sake that the sum of individual satisfactions may be maximized when incomes are equalized. But in this condition of income equality, if it be the best, must not market values set by the buyers and the resulting allocation of resources be, *ex hypothesi*, the best and most desirable? Is it not in direct contradiction with this whole line of reasoning to resume production of items that are not now in demand?

By our redistribution process we have now, it is assumed, reached the condition of maximum welfare, where the sum of individual satisfactions is maximized. Is it not illogical immediately to move away from it?

Surely, when we achieve the distribution of incomes which, it is claimed, maximizes the sum of satisfactions, we must let this distribution of incomes exert its influence upon the allocation of resources and productive activities, for it is only through this adjustment that the distribution of incomes is made meaningful. And when resources are so allocated, we must not interfere with their disposition, since by doing so we shall, as a matter of course, decrease the sum of satisfactions. It is then an inconsistency, and a very blatant one, to intervene with state support for such cultural activities as do not find a market. Those who spontaneously correct their schemes of redistribution by schemes for such support are in fact denying that the ideal allocation of resources and activities is that which maximizes the sum of satisfactions.

But it is clear that by this denial the whole process of reasoning by which redistribution is justified falls to the ground. If we say that, although people would be better satisfied to spend a certain sum on needs they are more conscious of, we deprive them of this satisfaction in order to support a painter, we obviously lose the right to argue that James's income must go to the mass of the people because satisfaction will thereby be increased. For all we know, James may be supporting the painter.[35] We cannot accept the criterion of maximizing satisfactions when we are destroying private incomes and then reject it when we are planning state expenditure.

The recognition that maximizing satisfactions may destroy values which we are all willing to restore at the cost of moving away from the position of maximal satisfaction destroys the criterion of maximizing satisfactions.

Are subjective satisfactions an exclusive standard?

Indeed, the foregoing discussion reaches beyond a mere refutation of the formal argument for income redistribution. Economists as such are interested in the play of consumer's preferences through the market, and in showing how this play guides the allocation of productive re-

[35] It is permissible to retort that the rich Jameses put great parts of their incomes to less laudable uses and to argue that the public powers, taking over the incomes of the Jameses, will do more for culture than the rich had done. There is a strong case here (compare what the princes did for the arts from the Renaissance to the eighteenth centrury, with the services rendered by the *bourgeois* rich in the eighteenth century); but it is to be noted that what comes into discussion now is redistribution of power from individuals to the State and not redistribution from the rich to the poor. Whether or not the State is better qualified than the rich to support the arts (and that very much depends on the nature of the government and the nature of the wealthy class), if the State's warrant for taking over the incomes of the rich is its mandate to maximize satisfactions of the national consumers, it is not entitled by that warrant to apply its takings to another object, thus moving away from the position of maximal overall satisfaction.

sources so that it comes to correspond with the consumer's preferences. The perfection of this correspondence is general equilibrium. It is perfection of a kind; and it is quite legitimate to speak of such allocation of resources as the best, it being understood that it is the best from the angle of subjective wants, weighted by the actual distribution of incomes. This understanding, however, is often forgotten: Many economists, notably Wicksteed, have argued that it is not the best, because it is skewed by actual distribution. The peril inherent in this correction is that its champions are apt to forget that the allocation of resources resulting from such distribution of incomes as appears to them most desirable is, precisely as before, the best only from the angle of subjective wants, weighted by the new distribution of incomes. Calling it the best without qualification implies a value judgment which equates the good with the desired, on Hobbesian lines. Now it is quite legitimate for the economist to deal only with the desired and not with the good. But it is not legitimate to treat the optimum in relation to desires as an optimum in any other sense. And that the allocation of resources in relation to desires should fail to be optional by other standards should not come as a surprise to us.

That a society which we may assume to have maximized the sum of subjective satisfaction should, when we survey it as a whole, strike us as falling far short of a "good society," could have been forseen by anyone with a Christian background or a classical education.

To the many, however, who were apt to think so much in terms of satisfactions that the "badness" of society seemed to them due to the uneven distribution of satisfactions, it must come as a most useful lesson that the outcome of this viewpoint leads them into an unacceptable state of affairs. The error must then lie in the original assumption that incomes are to be regarded solely as means to consumer-enjoyment. Insofar as they are so regarded, the form of society which maximizes the sum of consumer-enjoyments should be best, and yet it is unacceptable. It follows that incomes are not to be so regarded.

Redistributionism the end result of utilitarian individualism

There is no doubt that incomes are currently regarded as means to consumer-enjoyment, and society as an association for the promotion of consumption. This is made clear by the character of the controversy now proceeding on the theme of redistribution. The arguments set against one another are cut from the same cloth. It is fair, some say, to equalize consumer-satisfactions. It is prudent, the others retort, to allow greater awards to spur production and thereby provide greater means of consumption.

There is an American proverb: "The world is a pot and man a spoon in it." In this image, our two sides might choose slogans: an expanding pot with unequal spoons, or a static and possibly declining pot with equal spoons. But perhaps the world is not a pot and surely man is not a spoon. Here we have completely slipped away from any conception of the "good life" and the "good society." It is quite inadmissible to consider the "good life" as a buyer's spree or the "good society" as a suitable queueing up of buyers. And the redistributionist ideal represents a disastrous fall from socialism.

Socialism, before its disastrous decay into a new version of enlightened despotism, was an ethical social doctrine. And as such a doctrine must, to merit the double epithet, it looked to a "good society," which it saw as one wherein men would have better relations with one another and feel more kindly toward their fellows. This spirit seems to have evaporated from modern reformist tendencies. Redistributionism takes its cue wholly from the society it seeks to reform. An increased consuming power is the promise held out, and fulfilled, by capitalist mercantile society—so is it the promise of the modern reformer. And in fact the choice of right or left is to be finally regarded as not an ethical choice at all, but a bet. Taking, say, the period 1956–65, do we bet that redistributionism with its probable negative effect on economic progress will provide a majority with a higher standard of living than capitalism with its inequality? Or do we put our money—it seems the proper term—on the other horse?

There is no question of ethics here. The end-product of society is anyhow taken to be personal consumption: This is, under socialistic colors, the extremity of individualism. Finally, my probable consumption under one or the other system is to be my criterion. Nothing quite so trivial has ever been made into a social ideal. But it is wrong to accuse our reformers of having invented it—they found it.

What is to be held against them is not that they are utopian, it is that they completely failed to be so; it is not their excessive imagination, but their complete lack of it; not that they wish to transform society beyond the realm of possiblity, but that they have renounced any essential transformation; not that their means are unrealistic, but that their ends are flat-footed. In fact, the mode of thought which tends to predominate in advanced circles is nothing but the tail-end of nineteenth-century utilitarianism.

Lecture II

State Expenditure

Two views of income

Champions tilting for and against income redistribution do not have quite the same lady in mind. The redistributionist thinks of income essentially as a means to consumer-satisfaction, and he puts forward a case for equating satisfactions. To the anti-redistributionist, income is primarily a reward for productive services, and he is eager to scale rewards in such a way as to encourage a maximum flow of services.

Neither argument is completely solid on its own ground. The redistributionist, who starts out with a bold pretense of equating satisfactions, admits perforce that he cannot compare them and, after a pretense of measuring, bases his argument for income equalization upon his very ignorance. Nor is he in fact content with the allocation of productive resources brought about by the free use of equalized incomes; he controls the use of these equalized incomes so far as may be necessary to offset the effects of equalization upon the allocation of social resources.

The anti-redistributionist, on the other hand, clearly has a case for allotting incomes in such a way as to provide the greatest incentives, but it is quite untenable to claim that the existing distribution corresponds with the distribution he desires; consequently, the logic of his case, which he is seldom wont to follow, would lead him to a redistributionism of another inspiration, and pursued by means other, but no less bold, than that of his opponent. It may be worthwhile briefly to notice that this champion of maximum production may not always disagree with his adversary.

Taxation not purely disincentive

The point has been made a thousand times that heavy, rapidly progressive taxation has a deterrent effect upon enterprise. This is clearly illustrated in the case of the fortune-builder. Here is a single man whose enterprise over successive laps of time multiplies his earnings first from £400 to £2,000, then from £2,000 to £10,000, then from £10,000 to £50,000. With each lap he multiplies his gross income five times; with the first lap he multiplies his net income almost four times, with the second lap 2.7 times, with the third lap 1.4 times. Out of a first increase of £1,600 gross he keeps £962 10s., or more than one pound in two; out of his second increase of £8,000 gross he keeps £2,212 15s., or more than one pound in four; out of his third increase of £40,000 he keeps £1,474 10s., or one pound in twenty-seven! He actually gains less pounds the third time he multiplies his income fivefold than he gained when he did so the second time. It seems quite obvious that we have here rapidly decreasing returns for effort, which is psychologically a disincentive. Of course, to make such an assertion water-tight, we should have to study the pound-productivity function of our man at the various stages of his progress. It is logically possible that it costs him much less effort in a certain position to make £30 than it did to make £2 in a former position; and then it would seem to follow that the same effort in his last position, where he must abandon £26 out of £27 he makes, still nets him a little more than it did in the former position when two pounds made netted him one. It would then be impossible to speak of decreasing returns, and one should possibly speak of insufficiently increasing returns. However, in the case we have taken there is strong *prima facie* evidence that our fortune-builder is deterred from further effort by the relative insignificance of his reward.

Indeed, in addition to this psychological brake, there is an even more serious phenomenon. Our illustration is highly improbable in these days because our man will have been prevented from hoisting himself up so far. On his way, taxation will have taken such a toll as to prevent his rise, his accumulation of capital, and his entering into competition with formerly established businesses. But this is an aspect other than that with which we are at present concerned.

So much for the case for the disincentive effect of redistributionist taxation. But the incentive effect of such taxation, insofar as it strikes at the lower-middle layers of incomes, cannot in fairness be neglected. Heavy taxation has thrown on the labor market possessors of unearned incomes paying the standard rate (the depreciation of buying power further intervening), and also members of families formerly supported by one income earner whose income heavy taxation has made inadequate. In a great and varied number of cases, heavy taxation has impelled its middle-class victims to increased efforts in order to retain, in part at least, a former standard of life.

Thus, redistributionist policies cannot be called purely disincentive: They are not so all along the line. It can be claimed that while heavily progressive taxation tends to discourage people from becoming *entrepreneurs,* it tends on the other hand to stimulate to greater activity the existing middle classes, which must multiply their efforts to avoid sinking into an altogether different way of life. It may well, as a consequence, increase the importance of these classes in the national economy, and thus their claim to leadership. It seems, however, that on the working class the effect must be disincentive, because the share of lower incomes which is independent of productive efforts is increased. There seems to be little doubt about this result under pure redistribution. But redis-

tributionist policies in practice may work altogether otherwise. Insofar as redistributionist policies call upon the
healthy workers to bear the burden of the unfit, or the
bachelors to bear the burden of the children of others, as
in France, they deplete the disposable income of the
healthy and of the bachelor and have an incentive effect.
These are merely pointers to the fact that the argument
against redistribution on the grounds of maximizing national effort does not seem any more solidly based than
the argument for redistribution on the grounds of maximizing welfare.

Another view of income

These arguments, however, are far from embracing all
that can be said about income distribution. The concepts
of income as the means to consumer-satisfaction and as a
reward for productive effort are in economics complementary, but they do not exhaust the reality of income. It
is only if one pictures society as a kitchen-cum-hall stage
set, where the actors can be seen on the one hand broil-
ing some indistinguishable "stuff" which on the other
hand they absorb, that we can be content with these two
notions of income. But in fact, to keep to our theatrical
comparison, what we took for the stage is only back-
stage. True, the actors are busy producing the stuff that
they are also consuming, eating, spreading upon their
faces, turning into props, whatever you will; but this
only in order to strut upon the stage. In other terms, consumption is not the ultimum, the final outcome of production; it also can be regarded as mere means to the real
ultimum: human life.

Men's lives are surely to man as student the important
phenomenon in society, the thing of beauty or at least of

interest. Consumption is merely the means of supporting these lives. To the social philosopher interested in human beings it must seem absurd that one should be passionately interested in equalizing among these lives supplies of the "stuff," on the ground that absorbing the stuff is the stuff of life. It must, on the contrary, seem to him tragic, and a matter for intervention, that the stuff should fail either to support a life or to carry it through. To him, what is bad is that the stuff should run short for whatever course a life may take.

To abandon a long-drawn metaphor, incomes are not solely means to consumer-satisfaction nor incentive rewards, but they do contribute to human life and should perhaps be regarded chiefly as means to accomplishment.

Gnawing the income-bone

The notion of income as means to consumer-satisfaction assumes two things: that consumption is *asocial* and that it is *unproductive*. It must be asocial, be pleasurable or profitable to the income holder alone; under such conditions indeed there is no perceptible reason for allowing Primus more selfish satisfaction than Secundus. And it must be unproductive: Why should Primus make a trip to Italy and not Secundus? Why indeed, if both are merely bent on pleasure jaunts? But should Primus be a young architect seeking to familiarize himself with Renaissance designs, surely his tour is not to be set on the same footing as the pleasure jaunt of Secundus!

The notion of income as means to consumer-enjoyment implies that the individual, his day's work done, his debt to society discharged, retires to masticate his income-bone in seclusion, a selfish gastric process, leading nowhere.

But it is not so. Living is a social process. Our individual life is not for ourselves alone. A generous spirit will render many services to society outside his professional activities. A professor's open table may be a means of education superior to his lectures, or complementary to them. Individual income, socially consumed, is a means to such services. These are not accounted as productive services, because they are free. The misleading picture of national income takes into account only services on which a commercial price is put. This is blinding us to the destruction of values which are not commercialized.

Further, the metaphor of the income-bone ignores the salient fact that consumption is to a large extent necessary outlay to bring forth productive activities.

From the scrap-heap of discarded notions let us for a moment rescue the "iron law of wages," from which Marx derived his celebrated error that all the employer pays for is the cost of reproduction of the laborer's force. The "iron-law" wage just allows the laborer to keep fit for his task. If we focus our attention on such a wage we may properly state that it includes no net income and that only whatever the worker in fact receives over and above such a wage can be accounted net income. Acting upon this assumption, practically all fiscal systems allow a basic deduction from income, this being exempt from taxation.

Proceeding therefrom, we may be tempted to say that for all income recipients there is the same basic need to be met, above which net income begins, and this is in fact the prevailing system. This idea of identical basic needs has been encouraged by its evident truth in the case of our lower functions and by the consequent justifiable practice of food rationing.

But the reasoning is in fact very faulty: Keeping a man physically fit and keeping him fit for diverse social duties are not identical notions. The same basic expenditure on basic needs which keeps a common laborer fit for his job will prove inadequate to keep a Treasury official fit for his specific task.[1] Each specific task calls for "functional expenditure," which is in fact cost of production and should not enter into net income.[2]

Conflict of subjective egalitarianism and objective socialism

Let us provisionally set aside the first point we have made, namely, that individual incomes may in part be used for social consumption, may be the occasion of satisfaction to people other than their recipient, may perform a social function and indeed sustain the higher forms of civilization, which are dependent upon give and take, as opposed to buying and selling. We will for the moment concentrate exclusively upon our second point: that consumption is, to a certain degree, the condition of productive services.

It is certainly more expensive to train an acceptable doctor than an acceptable docker, and there is again a difference, though possibly a slighter one, in the expenses incurred in maintaining the one and the other fit for their diverse tasks. Such differences are understood by every-

[1] It is, of course, equally true and even plainer that the food allowance sufficient for an office worker or a shop clerk will not keep a miner or a docker fit for a task calling for a greater expenditure of physical energy. It is characteristic of the passion for equality which has ruled in Britain that such a clear claim should have aroused so much opposition.
[2] It is only the "surplus" of incomes which one can reasonably think of equalizing. Indeed, in the case of surpluses it is plausible to argue that more "surplus" is called for in the case of the most distasteful labors.

body, just as it is admitted that a docker needs more food than a clerk.

But if that is so, then a policy of rigorous equalization of gross incomes would impair the efficiency of those performing the higher functions—this being short for those functions which demand greater individual expenditure. This indeed was rapidly perceived in the early days of Soviet Russia: After a very brief spell of equality, inequality was reestablished, and so sharply that the scale of remunerations is much steeper than in the West. Nor is this at all puzzling. First, the difference in earnings must be sharpest where those performing the higher functions have no unearned incomes. In the West, we also find that the higher tasks need to be more highly rewarded as they pass out of the hands of classes possessing some unearned income, or as such income becomes negligible.

A second and more important consideration is that scaling must logically be steepest where the social product per head is lowest. In rich, advanced countries the gross national product is such as easily to meet the bare cost of both the higher and the lower talents, and the balance may go to better the lot of the latter. But in poor, backward countries the national product may be inadequate to meet properly, over and above the cost of the lower talents, the cost of a desirable volume of higher talents. It then happens that the cost of this *élite* is met only by stinting the masses, which steepens the scale and contrasts with the generosity toward the unfavored that tends to flatten the scale in the advanced countries.

The contrast is then due far less to social and political regimes than to differences in the degree of economic development. The more backward a country, the greater the need for productive talents to pull it out of its backwater, the greater the inducement to support these talents even at the cost of great hardship to the masses.

Indeed, social history teaches us that what we have of civilization was bought at an enormous cost, the *élites* from which we derive our culture having been supported by sweated masses—a subject on which Bakunin, among others, wrote most eloquent pages. Even in our day we meet the problem when we very properly concern ourselves with Asiatic or African populations. These can only progress through investment in *élites* as well as investment in machines. The present tendency is to provide such investments from foreign funds. But if western riches were unavailable, the choice would be between sweating their equivalent out of the mass of lower incomes or leaving matters as they are.

The "scientific" socialist, far more concerned with future social welfare than with the preferences of individual living beings, is thereby very prone to sweat investment out of the toiling masses and must therefore logically subscribe to that most effective form of investment, investment in the higher talents. The system does not differ essentially from that which obtained in the Middle Ages, when the life of all *élites* was drawn from land taxes on the laborers, except in this very important respect: that the forthcoming *élites* are expected to give an immediate *quid pro quo* to the masses by services in medicine, engineering, education, etc. Similarity to the medieval *élites* is indignantly denied on the ground that these failed to give the *quid pro quo*. The services of the Church are now held to constitute no such return; our ancestors, however, thought otherwise.

This point need not be labored; it is clear enough that progress is linked with the existence of *élites*, the production and upkeep of which are costly and the incomes of which could not be flattened out without great social loss.

Functional expenditures well received if charged to corporate bodies

The egalitarian trend notwithstanding, it is generally agreed that men fulfilling certain functions need considerable means and eventual amenities which fit them to render their specific services. But such expenditure is regarded in an entirely different light, depending on whether it is assumed by these men out of their incomes, or assumed for them by *ad hoc* institutions.

Let us imagine two scientists in the medical field, one of whom joins a great institution while the other goes into general practice. Public opinion will not dream of criticizing the lavish laboratories of the institute, its expensive library, nor even the possibly well-appointed canteen, the comfortable smoking-rooms, and the tennis courts provided to relax the nerves of the research worker. Nor will anyone dream of apportioning the many facilities provided per head, of estimating the cost of tools provided, or the cost of amenities offered, and no statistician will regard the individual income of the researcher as raised by these advantages.

On the other hand, our general practitioner will find it difficult to get expenses incurred in keeping abreast of scientific developments accepted as professional costs; and if he runs to smoking-rooms and tennis courts the plea that such nerve-soothing amenities are indirect costs will arouse indignation rather than command a sympathetic hearing—though indeed means of relaxation may be far more necessary to him than to his secluded colleague.

Here we come up against the feeling so prevalent in our day, that corporate bodies may do what individuals may not and that partakers in corporate existence may thereby enjoy privileges which would be denied them in their capacity as mere individuals.

The treatment of corporate bodies compared to that of families

Corporate bodies, *personáe fictae,* enjoy in our day a quite fantastic preference over real people. Taxation is but one of many fields in which this preference can be observed. It has occurred to no Chancellor of the Exchequer to tax public companies at a progressive rate on their gross incomes, as individuals are taxed. Taxation, bearing upon the inflow of receipts regardless of expenditures, would then unquestionably do away with so-called monopolies and giant structures of any sort: All would shrink to a becoming degree of smallness, not without a seismic liquidation of assets, a catastrophic fall in efficiency, and an immense decline in the national product.

Not only has this never been suggested, but even the milder measure of progressive taxation applied to gross profits *before* deductions for depreciation has found no advocates. It is regarded as a matter of course that taxation must bear only upon net income, arrived at by the deduction first of operating expenses and second of amortization allowances. And even this net income is taxed only at a proportional rate.

Thus, the profit-seeking enterprise has a treble advantage over the family, which is taxed at progressive rates and is not allowed to provide for depreciation of its assets or to deduct operating expenses. And yet the family performs in society no less important a function than the firm.

The firm produces the goods, the family produces the people. It is puzzling that the needs of the former should be so well understood by the law-makers and the needs of the latter so disregarded. It seems that law-makers can picture only the firm as an institution with a purpose and therefore respectable. The income recipient, on the other hand, his day's work done, is seen as going round the booths of a fair, blueing his rights to consumer-satisfaction. It is not realized that he is an entrepreneur in his own right. He marries, sets up a house, raises children, and, it is to be assumed, struggles to bring himself and his family to the greatest possible degree of accomplishment. His achievement is to be recognized as useful to society in that he fits himself and his descendants for their roles as producers; in this respect, it is an indirect contribution to the raising of national income. But the matter is not to be taken from that angle only: His achievement is far more than a contribution to *another* end, it is an end *per se*, it is *the* end of a "good society" or a major part of it.

It is quite incomprehensible that a breeder of dogs for the race-track should be allowed his costs, depreciation, etc., while the father of the family is not. It is as if the law-makers sympathized more with the purpose of the former, which is to sell dogs for the track, than with the purpose of the latter, which gives men to society—incidentally for soldiering and tax-paying.

It is incomprehensible to the point of scandal that public authority should facilitate the upkeep of a tawdry picture or variety theater, but not the upkeep of a great house, a thing of aesthetic and ethical value, out of which have come generations of the men who have made England what it is. Out of cinema takings, the wherewithal to preserve the cinema in its present state is deducted from taxable income. This is not so in the case of a home, and there is no reason for it other than the legislator's blind spot. It is not to be excused on the grounds that commercial ventures must be favored over family ventures, the former being of such a nature that no one would embark upon them were they as ill-treated as the latter; for non-profit-making institutions enjoy even better treatment than commercial ventures. The family is such an institution; but as a natural body it is denied the advantages afforded to artificial bodies.

Consumption expenditures as a form of national investment

Admittedly, it is impossible to disentangle from family accounts something which might be called the net income of a family. A net income can easily be arrived at in the case of firms because net income is precisely what they are out to obtain. But if something of the thoughtfulness which has gone into the appraisal of corporate needs was brought to bear on family needs, the cost of maintaining a home, of developing talents and so forth might certainly be taken into consideration. It is enough for our present purpose that they should be kept in mind.

The ideal of income equality is, then, seen to fail by the two standards: justice as between individuals, and social utility.

Let there be two physically similar families, A and B, the former having a much higher pattern of accomplishment than the second. It will then happen that the supposedly higher income of A will leave this family with much less actually available income than family B. All fractions of A's income will have been earmarked for constructive purposes. It is unjust to balk these purposes, causing a sense of frustration, in order to increase family B's capacity for aimless consumption.

From the angle of utility, the mass of consumption expenditures is surely to be regarded as the nation's current investment in the perfection of her people. Anything which increases the proportion of fair-booth consumption as against formative expenditure must be adjudged undesirable.

The foregoing argument admittedly cuts both ways: It works for the redistributionist insofar as redistribution cuts down the mere enjoyment of the rich in favor of the health of the poor. Let us by all means turn yachts into county council houses. But it works in the other direction as soon as redistribution cuts into the cultural expenditure of the middle classes to feed the amusement industries.

Purposeful expenditures the State's privilege

The case for productive consumption is so strong that all opinions coincide on this point. If leftism is unwilling to take account of productive consumption in its treatment of personal incomes, it is not out of indifference to formative expenditure, but because this is regarded as henceforth the State's business. There is no sympathy for the father who spends vast sums on his son's education, and they are not accepted as costs deductible from taxable income, because the father need not, and some would say should not, bear this expenditure. The State will see to it that the boy gets the education, if state auditors so decide. The expense, and the decision, are to be taken out of private hands. It does not matter that personal incomes are so amputated as to become incapable of bearing constructive costs. They need not do so, and more precisely they are not meant to. Let the income recipient spare himself the trouble, thus recuperating net income to squander; the public authority will fulfill such of these individual purposes as are found worthy.

This attitude tends to turn personal incomes into a sum made up of the means of physical support plus pocket money. The citizen thereby loses a fundamental social responsibility: that of contributing in his private capacity to the advancement of his dependents and of his surroundings. He is encouraged to become something like a maintenance man. Insofar as he adopts this attitude, equalization of incomes becomes justified. If surplus over mere cost of physical needs is to be spent at the races, why indeed should one have a greater surplus than the other?

While heads of families must perforce cease to provide accomplished and useful members of society and are shorn of their power to advance society by their individual efforts, the State assumes full responsibility. How does it discharge it, and at what cost?

It does not see to everything, and, for instance, fails to build up homes which are an education in themselves. It does, however, spend a lot of money, and in the process it destroys the incomes of the upper and middle classes without building up those of the working classes.

A high degree of taxation in all ranges

We have already made the point that a thoroughgoing and consistent egalitarianism would redistribute incomes equally and let subsequent effects take their course. If, in such circumstances, a number of social accomplishments went undemanded, the conclusion would seem to follow that such accomplishments had no place in the "society of equals."

We noticed that redistributionists turn their backs on so simple a course and keep up, or even greatly develop from public funds, services which the "society of equals" would not buy on a free market at anything like the costs assumed by the State.

The clipping of the upper- and middle-class incomes therefore necessitates an increase in public expenditure and in public taxation. We saw in the first lecture that nothing like the sums which seemed at first sight available from higher incomes were in fact capable of being redistributed, their contributions to the Treasury and to investment having to be deducted. But now a further most important deduction has to be made, insofar as the State proposes to restore out of public funds such formative expenditures as were previously borne by heads of families. Thus, a father is not to be spared sufficient income to cover the cost of sending his son to Paris to study painting, but the State may pay for it. It is out of the question to lessen a family's taxation so that it may keep up a historic mansion, but a curator may well be appointed with a proper remuneration.

Unless, indeed, all prevailing values be discredited, it is inevitable that the redistributionist State should assume the upkeep of these values. But with this further charge on its takings from higher incomes it has nothing left with which to swell the nether incomes. And in fact, burdened with its many tasks, it follows the redistributionist pattern only in its takings, not in its largesse.

At least, one may say, the vast sums which are ultimately wrung out of the upper and middle classes are made better use of than before, and such part of those expenditures as was not clearly justified is eliminated. Is this so?

The camouflage of personal expenditures

It is worth going into some detail as to the fate of a number of expenses which were formerly personal expenditures and which the new dispensation apparently does away with; in fact, they are pushed into the compartment of business or institutional expenses.

There was a time when businessmen would have scorned to charge the entertainment of business, or other, acquaintances to operating expenses, but this has become a common practice. The car has ceased to be the director's—it is the firm's. Lucky indeed is the businessman or, for that matter, the member of any corporate body. He is in a position to charge to the business or institution all costs which are in the least degree attendant upon his work, or can be so represented.

This is a consequence of the aforementioned privilege belonging to corporate bodies. Therefrom follows a considerable inducement to persons to become associate or dependent members of corporate bodies, thereby gaining rights of which they were not possessed as persons: a glaring inequality. The trend of our day is therefore toward the reproduction of the medieval situation: *Nul homme sans seigneur*. It is appropriate here to recall that the so-called Dark Ages began with the flight of individuals into the protection of lords or chapters and came to an end when the individual again found it to his advantage to set forth on his own. We live at a time when everything conspires to push the individual into the fold.

The destruction of free services

We have noticed that consumption is assumed in the prevailing doctrines to be both unproductive and asocial. We have discussed at some length the productive character of family consumption and seen that insofar as taxation makes productive expenditures difficult for the head of the family, such productive expenditures tend to be pushed on to corporate bodies or assumed by the State.

Let us now attend to the social character of individual, or family, expenditure. The modern statesman understands that engineers, chemists, and other such must be trained and kept in a state of fitness, and it is quite eager that the State should assume the cost of such people, quite willing that the corporate bodies for whom they work should charge as costs functional facilities and amenities provided to these valuable citizens.

But the individual's value to society does not lie exclusively in the professional services he renders. It would be a sorry society in which men gave nothing to their contemporaries over and above the services for which they are rewarded and which enter into the computation of national income. That would be no society at all. Often enough one has a frightening vision of such a society, when one sees in some suburban train tired men traveling back from the day's toil to the small house in which they will shut themselves up to eat and sleep until they travel back to the factory or to the office. At those moments one treasures what is left of society: warm hospitality, leisured and far-ranging conversation, friendly advice, voluntary and unrewarded services. Culture and civilization, indeed the very existence of society, depend upon such voluntary, unrewarded activities. They are time- and resource-consuming and costly. There seems to be little awareness among us that they have entered upon a precipitous decline.

This decline goes unnoticed in our age of figures, and indeed the phenomenon is paradoxically shown in statistics as an increase. This occurs insofar as previously unrewarded services come to be salaried and are therefore dignified into "output." The unpaid secretary of a club is not a producer, but he becomes so the moment he is paid. Cobden's lectures on free trade would not be accounted a service in the tally of national income, but the activity of a paid party agent is so accounted. Strangely enough, socialists, who dislike valuation by the market, have become dependent for their policies upon an intellectual technique which draws its validity entirely from the valuations of the market. Thereby services freely given have tended to be overlooked as against professional services. The consequences stretch very far: It has often been noted that a man and wife get worse treatment as such than they would as a combination of employer and housekeeper. In the field of public life, disregard of the value of free services works against the very principle of democracy.

Surely it is a most undesirable division of social labor which sets apart a class of public managers as against a mass of passive citizens who then are not truly citizens. Yet what else can happen if mere citizens are left no margin of resources to expend on public activity and at the same time come up against the competition of professionals? How could a Cobden of today fare in his campaign, faced as he would be by full-time employees of adverse interests? It is puzzling that private corporate interests should be allowed to count as legitimate costs propaganda for their special cause, while the citizen is allowed no margin of income with which to further his disinterested championship of the common weal.

The stripping of incomes goes so far that even hospitality tends to be discouraged. As a result of the State's assumption that consumption is *asocial* it tends to become so. The age of socialism turns out to be that in which men are most shut into their individual lives, most confined to their several paths.

Commercialization of values

An important component of socialism was the ethical revolt against the sordid motivations of a commercial society, where everything, so the saying went, was done for
money. It is, then, a paradoxical outcome of socialist policies that the services which were rendered without
thought of reward should be on their way to disappearance, a number of these activities being turned into pro-
fessions and therefore performed for a monetary reward.
Only very careless thinking can represent modern society
as one in which more and more things are freely given.
Services which are paid for in bulk by taxation are not
freely given. And how could they be, when the producers of these free services claim salaries equal or superior
to those which reward services that the individual buys
in the market? The only services which are truly free are
those which are rendered by individuals exacting no payment for them; and these are most manifestly on the
decline.

An unnoticed consequence of this development is that
demand rules far more imperiously in our society of today
than it did heretofore. Where there is no margin of leisure
and income to enable individuals to offer free services,
where all services can be offered only insofar as their performance is paid for, either by individual buyers or by the
community, there is no opportunity of proffering services
the want of which is not felt by a sufficient number of consumers or by the leaders of the community.

Let us take as an illustration the various investigations
into working-class conditions made in the nineteenth
century. Such work was at the time susceptible of being
rewarded neither by the commercial market nor by the
government. It was done at the cost of individuals such
as Villermé or Charles Booth, who thought it necessary to

focus public attention upon the sorry state of things. Their initiative has altered the course of history. But the very people whose politics have been shaped by the outcome of these investigations tend to make such individual moves impossible in the future. And had the institutions toward which we tend been active at the time, the lack of private and of public demand for such investigations, the lack of prospective gains on the market and of state credits earmarked for the purpose would have defeated the venture.

There is generally no market for new ideas. These have to be elaborated and set forth at the cost of the innovator or a few adepts. It is an arresting thought that the writing of Marx's *Das Kapital* was made possible only by Engels' benefactions out of untaxed profits. Marx did not have to sell his wares on the market, nor did he have to get his project accepted by a public foundation of learning. His career testifies to the social utility of surplus incomes. It is, of course, assumed by *Etatistes* of today that Marx under the new dispensation would benefit from ample and honorable public support. But it seems so to them because his idea is now an old one and is accepted as the prevailing prejudice of our time. An innovator as bold today as he was in his day would not get by the boards of control which administer public funds. Nor is this scandalous: It is not the business of those who administer the common chest to subsidize bold ideas. These have to be offered on the market for ideas by convinced venturers.

A redistribution of power from individuals to the State

Our examination of the redistributionist ideal in theory and practice has led us gradually away from our initial contrast between rich and poor toward quite another contrast—that between individuals on the one hand, and the State and minor corporate bodies on the other.

Pure redistribution would merely transfer income from the richer to the poorer. This could conceivably be achieved by a simple reverse-tax or subsidy handed to the recipients of lower incomes from the proceeds of a special tax on higher incomes. But this is not the procedure which has prevailed. The State sets up as trustee for the lower-income group and doles out services and benefits. In order to avoid the creation of a "protected class," a discrimination fatal to political equality, the tendency has been to extend the benefits and services upward to all members of society, to cheapen food and rents for the rich as well as the poor, to assist the well-to-do in illness equally with the needy. The cost of such services has soared in England, according to *The Economist*, to as much as £1,800 million per annum (*Economist*, 1 April 1950) and is quite incapable of being met by taxation of the well-to-do, the lopping off of all incomes above £2,000 yielding only £431 millions and of those above £1,000 only £784 millions. In fact, the public authorities, so that they may give to all, must take from all. And from the study made by the E.C.A. mission to the United Kingdom, it appears that lower-income families taken as a whole pay more into the exchequer than they draw from it.

The more one considers the matter, the clearer it becomes that redistribution is in effect far less a redistribution of free income from the richer to the poorer, as we imagined, than a redistribution of power from the individual to the State.

Redistribution an incentive to tolerating the growth of public expenditure

Public finance generally is a dull subject, but public finance in the first half of the twentieth century is entrancing: It has been revolutionized and in turn has been the means of a revolution in society. Out of many new aspects of public finance, the two most notable are, first, that it has been used to alter the distribution of the national income between social classes and, second, that the fraction of national income passing through public hands has enormously increased.

Another important novelty, the use of the Budget to stabilize the economy as a whole, follows from these two innovations and is intimately linked with them. The point I propose to make here is that avowed redistributionist policies have made possible the tremendous growth of taxation and public expenditure. The role played by the State in transferring incomes evidently entailed some increase in the volume of public encashings and payments, but this volume has grown out of all proportion to the needs of this function. Such growth has encountered only the weakest opposition; my argument is that a change of mind toward public expenditure has been induced by redistributionist policies, the greatest gainer from which is not the lower-income class as against the higher but the State as against the citizen.

Let us recall that in past phases of history the public authorities have found it difficult not only to increase their fractional share of national income but also, even in a period of rising real or nominal incomes, to retain the same proportion of this income as they previously enjoyed. The revolutions which occurred in Europe between 1640 and 1650—the English Revolution, the Naples Revolution, and France's abortive *Fronde*—all seem to be linked with resistance by taxpayers to government demands for more funds in view of the price revolution. The old attitude of taxpayers was ruled by the desire to keep the government down to its usual takings in nominal terms. It is then almost incredible that, notwithstanding the period of inflation we have gone through, governments of our century should have found it possible to obtain an ever-increasing fraction of the nations' real income.

Rulers, of course, tend to believe that the greater fraction of private incomes they can draw into the Treasury, the better for the community as a whole; for are they not the best judges of the common interest, which the individual, sunk in his selfish pursuits, cannot perceive? Taxpayers, however, have shown through the centuries little understanding of the superior capacity of their rulers to spend the citizen's earnings and have obdurately maintained their right to spend their incomes in their own manner.

Indeed, the subject's dislike of taxation has been the means of turning him into a citizen; it has provided the foundation of our political institutions. For what was Parliament originally if not a device to overcome the taxpayer's resistance? When I read today of a meeting of trade-unionists called together by the minister concerned to hear exhortations on productivity, I feel it must be something like the first parliamentary assemblies where representative taxpayers were told of the State's financial need. The grudging attitude of the people made the power of Parliament.

The taxpayers' front was then a bulwark of individual freedom and the cornerstone of political liberty. It is remarkable how this front has disintegrated in the last generation. This phenomenon, the political consequences of which have not yet attracted sufficient notice, is closely linked to redistributionist policies.

Resistance to taxation has not always been general; the late Stuarts and the late Bourbons kept small groups of pensioners who were all for increasing the load of the many. It was then made one of the cardinal principles of taxation that it was to spare no one and to benefit no special group. These principles were infringed early in this century when the State began to subsidize, albeit modestly, special services for specific groups; simultaneously a new mode of taxation was adopted, surtax, which bore only upon a minority. This was the thin end of a wedge driven into the solidarity of taxpayers. When war demanded a huge increase in the rate of income tax, this became quite unbearable for the poorer taxpayers, and deductions and allowances were necessary; these were compensated by an increasing steepness of surtax. Thus, the very heaviness of taxation made necessary a difference of treatment between the different income classes. When, at the end of the war, the State retained part of its taxation gains, it excused its avidity by providing net advantages out of taxation to the unfavored mass. Thus, a great increase in State takings and expenditure was made tolerable to the majority by some measure of redistribution, and the process was repeated and enhanced during and after the Second World War.

It is not meant to imply that any conscious policy of breaking down taxpayer's resistance by advantages given to the poorer majority was at any time pursued by anyone. But the fact is that all the steps in the swelling of the Budget were coupled with increasing inequality of treatment, deductions, allowances, and positive benefits for the citizens in the lower-income ranges. It is hardly necessary to recall that, however desirable the wearing down of income inequality, its achievement, through legislation which discriminates among citizens, tends to corrupt the political institutions. Even though such legislation results in a better society, its means of achievement through the support of a majority that benefits, as against a minority that submits unwillingly, injures the political spirit of the commonwealth. It is implied in the definition of the citizen that he lays no obligations upon fellow citizens which he does not himself assume. It may be said of such legislation that it improves those who suffer under it insofar as they promote or welcome it, but it can hardly fail to injure the spirit of those who are to benefit.

Redistribution incidental to centralization?

In our exploration, we have found ourselves repeatedly coming across centralization as the major implication of redistributionist policies. Insofar as the State amputates higher incomes, it must assume their saving and investment functions, and we come to the centralization of investment. Insofar as the amputated higher incomes fail to sustain certain social activities, the State must step in, subsidize these activities, and preside over them. Insofar as income becomes inadequate for the formation and expenses of those people who fulfill the more intricate or specialized social functions, the State must see to the formation and upkeep of this personnel. Thus, the consequence of redistribution is to expand the State's role. And conversely, as we have just seen, the expansion of the State's takings is made acceptable only by measures of redistribution.

We then may well wonder which of these two closely linked phenomena is predominant: whether it is redistribution or centralization. We may ask ourselves whether what we are dealing with is not a political even more than a social phenomenon. This political phenomenon consists in the demolition of the class enjoying "independent means" and in the massing of means in the hands of managers. This results in a transfer of power from individuals to officials, who tend to constitute a new ruling class as against that which is being destroyed. And there is a faint but quite perceptible trend toward immunity for this new class from some part of the fiscal measures directed at the former.[3]

This leads the observer to wonder how far the demand for equality is directed against inequality itself and is thus a fundamental demand, and how far it is directed against a certain set of "unequals" and is thus an unconscious move in a change of *élites*.

Envy a fundamental motive?

Let us in this connection make two relevant comments. The first is that income inequality has reigned in the most diverse societies at all times and has apparently been tolerated quite willingly. The second is that "unequals" have seldom been other than political rulers or, more generally speaking, persons whose private and public life were lived in a glare of publicity, figure-heads.

The first comment tends to dispel the idea that human nature revolts against inequality of means. Quite the reverse, it accepts it so habitually that Pareto thought inequality was at all times and everywhere expressed by the same function, with much the same parameters. Though the latter has been disproved, the very fact that the idea could be adduced by so learned a man testifies at least that the fact of inequality, and very pronounced inequality, is universal.

---

[3] Such immunity has already been afforded to the international bureaucracy.

The second comment is the most pregnant one. During the whole range of life of commercial society, from the end of the Middle Ages to our day, the wealth of the rich merchant has been resented far more than the pomp of rulers. The ungrateful brutality of kings toward the financiers who helped them has always won popular applause. This may perhaps be related to a deep feeling that individuals have no business being rich by themselves and for themselves, while the wealth of rulers is a form of self-gratification for the people who think of them as "my" ruler.

It is noticeable in this respect that the French Communists clubbed together to offer their leader Thorez a £4,000 car, and on his fiftieth birthday a quite formidable array of presents. This has been unintelligently mocked as contradictory to Communist ethics, and people have expected the beauteous car to injure the popularity of the Communist leader. Not so. The conduct of Thorez's followers is the natural behavior of men toward the leaders they accept. Far from being basely envious, as they are represented, the people have always been most generous of their scanty means toward those they think of as their betters and their chiefs. It is as if some obscure instinct of our species warned us that we must pamper our higher types, variants whose needs are greater than those of the median type. Let us prove that we are here on the right track by thinking of the protective fondness of the people for champions. They know that these champions are at the same time excellent and most fragile; and they wax angry when they feel that champions do not enjoy the best conditions. This is the characteristic attitude of the people.

This observation overthrows the common concept of members of the aristocracy as those who, by virtue of their strength, carve out for themselves a large portion of this world's goods. True aristocracies have never enjoyed an aristocratic status because they are strong—this Darwinian concept is inadequate; true aristocracies have been willingly favored by the people, who sensed that excellent types of mankind, in any realm, needed special conditions, and they have always delighted in granting them such conditions.

If the richer classes of our day do not benefit from such an attitude, it is because they do not seem excellent to the people of our day. The film-star or the crooner is not grudged the income that is grudged to the oil magnate, because the people appreciate the entertainer's accomplishment and not the entrepreneur's, and because the former's personality is liked and the latter's is not. They feel that consumption of the entertainer's income is itself an entertainment, while the capitalist's is not, and somehow think that what the entertainer enjoys is deliberately given by them while the capitalist's income is somehow filched from them.

The *bourgeois* has two deep convictions which lead to his undoing. He feels that he owes his income to no favor, but to his own, or his family's, efforts; and he feels that he is free to enjoy it in his own, generally secretive, way. This is precisely the reverse of the attitude which justifies exceptional income in the eyes of the people. They want to feel that exceptional income is their gift, and they demand that beneficiaries thereof shall make a gallant spectacle.[4]

---

[4] Another point perhaps deserves a brief mention. It may be held surprising that wealth differentials should be most bitterly resented in a market society, where fortunes accrue to those who have most promptly sensed and most adequately served the desires of the public. The "new rich" might be regarded with especial favor, having been hoisted to their position of vantage by the consumer's own appreciation of values. Yet the hierarchy which results from men's decisions as buyers seems to them as citizens the most inacceptable, and those superiorities which are the outcome of their daily behaviors are the least palatable. This offers ample food for thought, far beyond our subject.

I do not propose to sum up what has been rather a circumgyration around the concept of redistribution than an argument. Let me only underline that to whatever extent we feel that the uplifting of the least favored members of our society is called for, this is not logically bound up with the demand for equalization of incomes. The latter concept has been seen to lack any secure basis: It is unclear in idea and in its destructive aspect a transient rather than a fundamental feeling. The method of so-called redistribution through the agency of the redistributing State and its outcome, the favoring of corporate bodies over individuals, seem to us to pertain to a vast evolutionary process which will not result in equality, and in which the egalitarian ideal is put to work, in all good faith, for ends other than itself.

Appendix

The Potentialities of Pure Redistribution

The purpose of this appendix is to explore the potentialities of pure redistribution of incomes. Pure redistribution is defined as follows. Let h be a maximum income and H be the number of incomes exceeding this maximum; let the total amount of such incomes be $Hh + S$. S, or the sum of which this class of income holders can be shorn while leaving each of them in possession of an income amounting to h, we call surplus over the ceiling. Let a be a minimum income and A be the number of incomes falling short of this minimum. Let the total of such incomes be $Aa - L$. L is the sum which would have to be added to bring such incomes to the minimum level: We shall call it lack. Pure redistribution then is the filling out of the lack L by the application thereto of the suplus S. And our design here is to discuss the equation of L with S.

Pure redistribution as defined above seems to be the most exact enactment into the social structure of redistributionist feeling insofar as it addresses its disapproval simultaneously to insufficiency and to excess of incomes. When the lectures were delivered, it seemed relevant to investigate whether, in the social reality of today, the correction of "excessive" incomes could remedy "insufficient" incomes. The result of rough calculations to that effect are alluded to in the lectures and justified in the following exposition. But I feel it incumbent upon me to say that, having repeatedly returned to this study since then, I have grown increasingly aware of the difficulties attending any discussion of actual distribution. It is doubtful whether we may claim to know what the distribution of incomes is in fact (and those who provide us with what data we possess recommend in this respect a caution which is seldom shown); it is also doubtful whether we have any clear notion of "individual income." The difficulties will unfold themselves in the course of this discussion. Indeed, their gradual unfolding may well be the main justification of this exploration.

This is to be at the same time a concrete and an ideal discussion. It is concrete in the sense that we shall base it on concrete data—namely, incomes in the United Kingdom for 1947–48, data for which are given in the 91st Report of the Commissioners of Inland Revenue. We are greatly indebted to the Director of Statistics and Intelligence of the Inland Revenue for an extension of these data and for invaluable help in interpreting them. Mr. F.A. Cockfield is, however, in no way responsible for the errors in our logic or conclusions.[1]

The discussion, on the other hand, is ideal in the sense that we assume whatever redistribution we choose to try out as presenting no practical difficulties and as having no effect upon the volume of activity.[2]

Our task, then, seems very simple. We choose a minimum income, or floor. Therefore, a is given. We know how many incomes are beneath this floor, that is, we know A; we know the aggregate of such incomes and thus by how far this aggregate falls short of Aa. We then know our lack L. We therefore know how much we want S to be, since it is to be equated with L. We can try diverse values of h, different ceilings, till we find one which yields us the desired surplus.

---

[1] Advantage has been subsequently taken of the 92nd Report. These "blue books," as they are referred to in the course of this note, were preferred to the "white books" on income and expenditure because they afford more detailed data.

[2] Here we have even disregarded the effect upon investment.

Redistribution of pre-tax or post-tax incomes?

We may proceed to our objective by two different courses. When one thinks of redistribution, one is apt to picture it as occurring somehow before taxation, as if a special tax were levied upon arising incomes to even them out, leaving them to bear taxes in their new state. But in that case the exchequer suffers a great loss. Let us state it quite clearly: from the H incomes which we shall declare to be above ceiling, the exchequer takes in tax and supertax a total sum T. If such incomes are reduced to the ceiling h, the exchequer will obtain from them only whatever h incomes pay. From the whole surplus which will have been transferred to the below-the-floor income recipients, it will get practically nothing. Its loss will then be considerable. On a rough calculation, it appears that the setting of the ceiling at £2,000 and the redistribution of surplus might cost the exchequer a third of the present total yield of income tax. If we do not want to restrict accordingly the activities of the State, we have to make up this loss to the exchequer.

Some will say that the State, under a new distribution of income, will have to spend less for the least fortunate. But if so, the sums added to their incomes should not be counted as a net gain, and the services which they are to lose have to be offset against their gain in incomes. Indeed, if one asserts that the services which the State may cease to provide, to the tune of its loss in direct taxation, are services formerly benefiting the recipients of redistribution, one is in fact saying that the recipients' net benefit will be nil.

Consequently, it is incumbent upon us if we redistribute surplus before taxation to levy new taxes upon less than ceiling incomes to compensate the exchequer. In order to avoid this complication, it seems a better course to think of income redistribution as occurring logically

after taxes have been deducted, if chronologically simultaneously with taxation. Thus, we can think of our floor
as a floor of net incomes, of our ceiling as a ceiling of
net incomes.

A rough calculation

Let us then start on our venture. We set £250 as our
floor of net incomes, a convenient figure because it is
used as a dividing line in all available statistics. The
questions we must answer to ascertain our lack are:
How many post-tax incomes are there beneath this
floor, how much do they amount to, and therefore by
how much do they fall short of that number times 250?
Our first difficulty is that our only guide to that number
of incomes is afforded by the blue book, which, however, lists only the incomes above the exemption limit.
Thus we have, for incomes assessed in 1947–48, a total
of 10½ million incomes beneath £250 but above £120,
amounting to 1,995 millions,[3] and thus falling short by
£630 millions.

---

[3] The calculations are based upon the figures in this extension of table
32 in 91st Report of the Commissioners of Inland Revenue.

Range of Net Income	Nos.	Net Income	
£ 120–150	2,030,000	£m	275
150–250	8,470,000		1,720
250–500	8,740,000		2,950
500–1,000	1,378,000		896
1,000–2,000	320,000		427
2,000–4,000	58,500		156
4,000–6,000	3,430		14.6
Over £6,000	70		.4
	21,000,000		6,439
		Personal Tax	1,086
		Gross Income	7,525

Here we have a clear figure but quite obviously inadequate: It leaves out of account the incomes beneath the exemption level, which presumably stand in greatest need of being raised (this is to be qualified later on). We do not know either the number or aggregate amount of such incomes. Consequently, we do not know by how much we are to raise our figure of 630 millions. It is, however, plain that this figure provides at least a minimum estimate of our lack. And therefore it also provides a minimum estimate of the surplus to be obtained from higher incomes.

If we set the net income ceiling at £2,000, do we obtain a surplus of 630 millions? Far from it. Post-tax incomes above £2,000 amounted for the year considered only to 171 millions. Reducing them each to £2,000 only would have yielded no more than 47 millions. In the same manner, incomes above £1,000 amounted in all to 598 millions. Reducing them to £1,000 each would have yielded 216 millions.

We must descend to a £500 ceiling in order to obtain a surplus of £614 million, which is almost equivalent to our stated lack. The aggregate net income of taxpayers enjoying more than £500 is £1,494 million. The number of such income recipients is 1,760 thousand. An allowance of five hundred to each works out to £880 million. Hence an available surplus of £614 million.

Thus, working from a plainly undervalued estimate of the lack to be filled, we find that even so the required amount cannot be obtained by the sponging-off of "excess incomes," without setting a ceiling far lower than anyone seems willing to contemplate.[4]

[4] Whether assessed incomes fail to take into account some advantages accruing to those enjoying property or tenure (public or private) is another point. It is obvious that advantages which do not fall under the definition of income become more valuable as taxation of incomes grows more severe. In the case of redistribution of property (which lies outside our subject), the advantages of tenure become all important.

The significance of individual income

The foregoing results are very crude and whet the appetite for information. First, one would like to have even
more precise information as to the actual distribution of
incomes.[5] Second, we cannot rest content in ignorance of
what takes place beneath the exemption limit. How many
subterranean incomes are there which we would want to
lift? This question forces us to consider the nature of such
small incomes.

Among them are to be found the incomes of state pensioners, either single or married, or those of maiden la-
dies living from a small investment. In such cases, these
incomes support totally one life or two lives, perhaps
even more. But in this category lie also the incomes of
juveniles residing with their families, and those of members of the armed forces whose vital needs are covered by
the organization to which they belong.

Obviously, it would make no sense to think of raising a
juvenile living with his parents to a floor of £250 while
we would be content to leave his father and mother, with
possibly younger children, at the same £250 level. This
simple remark shows us that what we are really concerned to ascertain is not indeed how many individual
incomes there are beneath the exemption limit, but how
big is the population which lives from such incomes. We
come to think in terms of social groups. In the same manner, we would want to know what is the total population
living from less than £250 incomes.

[5] Britain is the country which has to date far and away the best information. Even so the *National Income and Expenditure* paper admits that
some 13% of the total income accruing to persons could not be allocated to particular ranges of incomes. M. Dudley Seers has recently attempted such allocation. From his studies it appears that their incor-
poration would not alter the distribution of incomes very significantly.

It seemed to me when the lectures were given that these questions could be answered by use of the residual method: The incomes declared would show, by the allowances and deductions claimed, how many people were supported by them. The necessary data were not then available in convenient form; but they are now by a most happy initiative of the Director of Statistics and Intelligence of the Inland Revenue. They can be found in table 87 of the 92nd Report.

It appears from this table, to my reckoning, that no less than 46 million people are supported by the 20,750,000 incomes above the exemption limit.[6]

Since the number of dependents may be underestimated, as we are warned, because of failure of people not liable to tax to claim all the allowances due to them, it seems that only a small portion of the population (especially when the armed forces are deducted) fails to be covered by these incomes. It therefore seems proper to lump this remnant with the income recipients in the 135/250 class and to take this population as a whole.

It seems, therefore, that we committed a far smaller error than we believed in neglecting this group. Let us do so again in a new calculation, the principle of which is as follows: Assuming that we now know the number of people supported by incomes in the 135/250 class, let us find by how much the total income of this class would have to be raised to bring the income per head on a level with the income per head of the 250/500 class. From the table referred to, we find 22.8 million people living from incomes in the 250/500 class; and the income per head comes to £136.9 pretax and 130 post-tax. In the 135/250

[6] This applies to the year 1948–49 when the exemption limit was £135. The detail as I find it is (in thousands): 10,381 single persons and 20,738 married people, with a total of 3,480 dependents and 11,575 children.

class, we find 16.2 million people, and the income per head is 104.3 pre-tax and 102.5 post-tax. Pre-tax equalization would then call for an amount of 528 millions,[7] to which something of course should be added in view of the disregarded remnant.[8]

Actual redistribution is oblique

To me the most surprising outcome of these clumsy calculations is that the sums involved are so small, relative to those which pass through the hands of the State. One is left wondering how far the formidable afflux of finance into the public coffers has in fact gone to the raising of nether incomes and whether greater results in that direction might not have been achieved if this purpose had not been involved with that of increasing the role of the State.

On the other hand, it is also striking to find that even such relatively small sums as we have named cannot be found by lopping off the tops of the higher incomes. It is not from "the rich" that the sums called for could be obtained, it is not indeed from the rich that the vast social expenditures made to date have been obtained.

It is enough to note that the total actual takings in direct taxation from the incomes of over £2,000 (£419 million) are inferior to the food subsidies alone, and even more inferior to the social expenditures of the State, however narrowly one wishes to limit the notion of social expenditure.

---

[7] The classes referred to are here pre-tax classes. In the case of lump groups, post-tax equalization seems inconceivable.

[8] The author begs to be excused for such naïve efforts in a field which properly belongs to experts.

Consequently, redistribution in practice is not "vertical," it is "oblique"; it is far more the horizontal translation of incomes than vertical descent, and the element of vertical descent plays a greater psychological than financial role. The idea that the sums which pass out of the State's hands come from above is true only as regards a very minor fraction; and it serves to obscure the fact that for the most part the buying power which is redistributed comes out of the same social layers as receive it.

Index

The text of this book was set in Palatino, designed in 1948 by the German type designer and calligrapher Hermann Zapf. To Zapf, "Type is the tie or ligature between author and reader." Palatino was the first of Hermann Zapf's typefaces to be introduced to America. It is distinguished by its broad letters and vigorous, inclined serifs.

This book is printed on paper that is acid-free and meets the requirements of the American National Standard for Permanence of Paper for Printed Library Materials, Z39.84, 1984 ∞

Book design by Hermann Strohbach, New York, New York
Editorial service by Custom Editorial Productions, Inc., Cincinnati, Ohio
Typesetting by Alexander Typesetting Company, Indianapolis, Indiana
Printed and bound by Worzalla Publishing Company, Stevens Point, Wisconsin